ANNE KRÜGER-DEGENER

25 Ways to Make Your Horse Happy

Essential Skills and Unique Tools for Making Training and Performance Fair and Fun

TRAFALGAR SQUARE

First published in the United States of America
in 2025 by
Trafalgar Square Books
an imprint of the Stable Book Group
32 Court Street, Suite 2109
Brooklyn, NY 11201
www.trafalgarbooks.com

Originally published in German as *Glücksschmiede für Pferde*.

Disclaimer of Liability
The author and publisher shall have neither liability nor responsibility to any person or entity with respect to any loss or damage caused or alleged to be caused directly or indirectly by the information contained in this book. While the book is as accurate as the author can make it, there may be errors, omissions, and inaccuracies.

Trafalgar Square Books encourages the use of approved safety helmets in all equestrian sports and activities.

Trafalgar Square Books certifies that the content in this book was generated by a human expert on the subject, and the content was edited, fact-checked, and proofread by human publishing specialists with a lifetime of equestrian knowledge. TSB does not publish books generated by artificial intelligence (AI).

ISBN: 978-1-64601-225-1
Library of Congress Control Number: 2024949534

Photo credits: All photographs by Anna Auerbach/Kosmos, except pp. 91, 92, 93, 97 left, 97 right, 98 (Horst Streitferdt/Kosmos), pp. 12 and 146 (Anne Krüger-Degener), p. v (Nadine Harms), and p. 14 (Thomas Ix), with an illustration by Shutterstock/Bokica.

German editor: Birgit Bohnet
Translation into English: Gabriele Popp, MD
English editor: Sarah O'Neill
Cover design: RM Didier
Interior design concept: Peter Schmidt Group GmbH, Hamburg
Interior design and typesetting: Atelier Krohmer, Dettingen/Erms

Printed in China
10 9 8 7 6 5 4 3 2 1

☞ *Contents*

PREFACE

I had to smile as I read the title of this book. First and foremost: WE are the master of our horses' fate. It is so important that we never forget this, because it is our responsibility to make sure that our horses are healthy and happy!

All of us communicate with our horses both consciously and—unfortunately—often unconsciously. We communicate verbally and non-verbally, with our body language and with how we move in a horse's space or allow them to move into ours.

Horses want to understand us, and they want to please us. They love to be recognized for who they are, and they love to be praised. Over the years, I have enjoyed learning what it means to become friends with the horses I get to work with. The emotions and the love they reflect back to me provide a rich foundation for our work together.

Reading this inspiring book gave me a lot of food for thought. "Dressage or liberty work doesn't mean training circus tricks. Dressage means communicating." I have noticed that it is not as easy for me to communicate clearly with my horses as I once thought it would be. At least not from the ground—I am (as with most things) still learning. However, like Anne, I have already internalized the rules of playful consistency in the saddle.

Working with your horse should be fun, and the time we get to spend with these marvelous creatures should be seen as a gift.

I was drawn to my barn as I read this book, to practice the topics discussed in these pages with love and joy, together with my horses. This is exactly what I wish for you: Be the master of your life and forge ahead—creating happiness for you and your horses!

Sincerely yours,
Jessica von Bredow-Werndl

Jessica von Bredow-Werndl

DREAM JOB: BUILDING HAPPINESS —*The Path to Becoming a Team*

WELCOME TO MY WORKSHOP

What did you want to be when you were little? Did you want to be a lawyer, a veterinarian, or a writer? Did you think about becoming an artist, or a riding instructor, or a youth coach? Did you want to become whatever it was you had picked because it would make you money—or because you wanted to be someone who creates happiness? And, deep in your imagination, hidden beneath all the demands of society, could that still be what you really want?

My job is to build happiness—happiness tailored to individual horses and their riders, carefully crafted, much like a farrier shapes a perfectly fitted shoe for each individual hoof. This is my passion, not only for horses but for their humans, and for their dogs and other animals as well. It's my dream job, and I love it. It's an occupation that can cultivate, restore, and repair happiness. In fact, it's so much more than work: it's a creative endeavor that brings beauty to your partnership with your horse and makes the entire team happier. Do you want an apprenticeship in my workshop? Join me!

First, I would like to show you my tools and how they should be used. Then, we will talk about the "raw material" you will be working with, and how to recognize and avoid potential pitfalls. It will be my responsibility during all this time to not only teach you the practical skills you need, but to make you fall in love with what we do. Only when you love what you do with a passion will your creativity develop fully, and this is when your goals become attainable.

Welcome to my workshop—together, let's work to build happiness.

Anne Krüger-Degener

"The more we care for the happiness of others, the greater our own becomes."

—The Dalai Lama

THE TOOLS

THE FOUR PILLARS OF MY SYSTEM FOR BUILDING HAPPINESS AND TRAINING IN HARMONY (HARMONILOGIE®)

1. Responsiveness
2. Rewardability
3. Attention-shifting
4. Acceptance of the aids

Why are these tools so important? Because they are the basis for a successful dialogue that establishes the correct exchange of information, be it in riding, driving, or handling on the ground. Whatever it is you want to accomplish with your horse, these four tools will be required—always.

It doesn't matter which species you are working with; I always remember them and use them.

The goal of my system is to be a team with any animal in training.

In order to learn how to communicate with them, it's worthwhile to watch and listen to our horses.

THE THREE ELEMENTS OF EACH PILLAR

For each pillar of my system for training in harmony, there are three elements: three for responsiveness, three for rewardability, and so forth. The system is extremely logical and simple to apply. Once you've learned it and can apply it, you only need to know one more thing—the six functional patterns—in order to read a horse's behavior. You will understand how to exchange misunderstanding for understanding and you will see your horse's expressive behavior clearly.

NATURE'S NATIVE LANGUAGE

You will learn to ask your horse questions and let him know you understand his responses. For this to work, you must communicate in his language. Horses tend to communicate using body language far more often than they use vocalization. I'll show you how to recognize these means of communication and how to use them yourself. You'll learn how you can regulate and activate your horse, and how to stay within, demand, and give space. You'll see why this common ground is the basis for a good partnership.

My system doesn't translate human language and psychology for animals; instead, it translates the communication patterns of animals for us. Horses use space and timing very precisely. They know how much distance to keep from other horses, when it's a smart move to drop their heads or present their shoulders, and when to chew and move away. Our beloved horses have an excellent sense of the space available to them, and they move within it with ease.

Humans don't usually use space this way; instead, we rely primarily on spoken language, with a complex vocabulary for things both real and imagined, concrete and abstract. Horses have none of our ability to think abstractly, but they are often far more aware of our state of mind than we realize.

A horse can feel tension in a human; he can smell stress hormones, and can recognize the intentions in a movement long before the movement is completed. In a stressful situation, a horse immediately assesses his running speed, his escape routes, and the odds of confrontation. And while we stand there agonizing over a situation, pondering our problems and our questions, from the horse's perspective, the misunderstanding has already been established. We can learn to communicate with horses if we can learn the way they speak. If we're unwilling to try, we will never be able to fully develop a true partnership with a horse. Having said that, it doesn't matter which discipline you work in with your horse, nor does it matter whether your horse is big or small, young or old; all horses speak the same language.

Learn to use a horse's means of communication, and to understand and categorize your horse's expressive behavior. Only then can communication between horse and human make sense and create a clear exchange of information, which leads to solutions—and to trust.

TRUE BONDING IS THE KEY TO HAPPINESS

Communicating with each other, not only by creating deep trust in the horse but also by feeling it yourself, creates a bond. You need to know why trust is so important and how you can build or repair it. This part of training in harmony is, in my mind, the most beautiful work you can accomplish (page 88).

THE PATH AHEAD

Join me as I work with a wide variety of horses and riders. Experience with me the concrete steps these teams have taken. You will probably see yourself in at least a few of these situations. I have included several videos where I not only hope to explain to you how to build a happy relationship with your horses, but to excite and empower you to do so. I'm going to do everything I can to make this work into your dream job.

Since this system simply uses nature's native language, it isn't complicated. It's knowledge that we all already have within us, somewhat buried by evolution. Rather than learning this new language, perhaps you'll find yourself "remembering" a language that feels like it's already yours.

"I often ask myself what the purpose of life is. I conclude that it is to be happy."

—The Dalai Lama

TRUE COMPREHENSIO

—Answering the Horse's Questions

COMMUNICATION REQUIRES CLARITY

Trust is a fragile construct, a tender thing that needs constant nurturing. Once destroyed, it is difficult to rebuild. Trust has two aspects:

1. Trust in oneself: self-confidence. As a coach, I have to keep working on this even with my two-legged customers.
2. Trust in your partner: this determines the quality of your relationship.

There is a symbiosis between these two parts; each can strengthen or weaken the other. The key to building a successful connection between them is the bond we work to create. We will explore this more starting on page 84.

Real trust begins with harmony.

A BLAME-FREE SPACE

Another key piece we need is understanding—not in the sense of literal comprehension, but in the sense of empathy and compassion. We also need an unambiguous way to communicate. This requires more than just understanding, of either kind. It demands the use of a clear training system to establish a smooth means to exchange information.

Misunderstandings between people and horses often happen when emotions run high; genuine listening is no longer possible and important signals are ignored. Feeling and expressing mutual respect has taken a back seat. In these instances, it can be easy to look for something to blame. This is a very important moment—there is a big black trap door opening up under you on the path to happiness, and you need to make sure you don't fall in.

You know what it's like: when you want to say something, but can't get your message across because the other person already thinks they know what you are about to say. You know the feeling of being misunderstood. You may have had the experience of having statements or feelings attributed to you that are not yours; it's frustrating.

With mutual trust, difficult lessons are safely and easily learned.

Horses and humans often talk past each other. We can change that when we improve our understanding of each other, when we learn to listen with all our senses, and when we ask questions. This level of understanding creates harmony on the ground and leads to success in the saddle. Learn to listen like a scientist. Observe your horse like a biologist. Keep track of what you have noticed. Learn to tell what is actually there, not what you wish was there. But also learn to tell what is not there but should be. Get involved in this journey of discovery.

WHEN IN DOUBT, THE HORSE WAS RIGHT

If you're certain you know exactly what the horse's behavior means and you still can't solve the problem you're experiencing, then ask the horse slower, friendlier, and quieter questions. Let someone film you, even in slow motion; watch the video, and ask yourself whether your language was clear and understandable for your horse. If there's any doubt, you should always decide the horse was right, and learn to balance dominance with compromise.

Trust is the basis of all feelings, and the greatest proof of love.

Trust is the most important element in the training of young horses.

Question: What do I have to change so that my horse can understand me better? You have to read, you have to study, you have to develop correct timing, and you have to work calmly with him. All this will lead you to your goals. You should fall in love with the idea of slowly developing your horse instead of thinking you can operate him like a machine. The difference between these approaches is that you will have to accept incorrect responses once in a while, as long as the overall trend goes in the right direction. The best example is the canter under the saddle: young horses, in the beginning, often have trouble recognizing the signal for starting the canter on the right lead. All they know is that they need to balance their body so they will not fall down. Hence, they might start the canter with the wrong lead, in counter canter, or canter on one lead in the front and with another in the back in an uncoordinated fashion. Some might buck, rear, or stand still—all incorrect responses from the human perspective, but perfectly reasonable responses from the horse's point of view. From at least six different plausible responses, the horse must choose the correct one. It is perfectly reasonable for a young horse to try some other possible answers before finding the right one.

Luckily, most horses find the correct response quickly, especially when they are supported by a good rider. However, there are some horses that don't have an easy time finding the correct answer right away, possibly because of their mental aptitude, physical development, or emotional state. Due to all of this, serious misunderstandings can occur. The skillful rider will develop the horse with care, regardless of whether the horse starts out the canter correctly, responding positively whenever the horse *tries*. The good trainer identifies the correct response for the horse using her own balance, with increasing strength if needed, and later associates it with a clear signal.

It is our job to recognize whether an error is a defensive behavior or a failure to understand (page 25). You can also learn to separate the reason for a mistake from the origin of the behavior to best help your horse learn from the misunderstanding. Even specific individual misbehaviors can have multiple causes.

A CASE STUDY

Violetta was an eight-year-old mare with very little training. She was a tense, "thin-skinned" horse with lightning-fast reactions. The young lady that brought her to me showed me her bridle, telling me she really didn't like the bit. I noticed how far away she was standing from her horse, and that made me suspect that there might be more to it. Both horse and owner stood there, tense and unblinking.

I looked at the bridle. It was a good piece of equipment, well cared for. As I approached the mare and reached out to pat her, her already huge eyes got even bigger, and she threw her head up in the air. "All right, then," I told the mare, "I will just look at you." As I stepped closer and put my hand on her neck, her skin started twitching and she held her breath. Even her owner stopped breathing. "I told you, she does not like that bridle," the owner told me again.

I started to rub Violetta's neck. She was so tense that she felt like concrete under my hand. But because she would be staying with me now for training, I had time to get to the bottom of this. She clearly didn't like to be bridled or touched on the head. When I tried, she danced around and almost piaffed in the cross ties, her tail swishing the whole time. This was going to be a project that would have to start at minus ten and work to even get to zero. But I was convinced that it was only a misunderstanding that had driven this young woman and her horse apart.

Training a horse holistically creates trust in the relationship.

Anticipatory Defense

I will explain what defensive behavior is and what it means on page 25. Let me just say this here: It is one of six traits that every living being has. It seems to be a survival mechanism, but it can cause misunderstandings. Defensive behavior does something to us emotionally, physically, and cognitively. It touches us. It might be caused by feeling rejected, fearful, or intimidated, or because we are unsure of our own actions. Defensive behavior can easily take control of us.

This beautiful liver chestnut mare had a very unique penchant for defensive behavior. She got tense at the drop of a hat, and didn't want to be touched much at all. When she held her breath, all the horses in the barn held their breath. It was as if she was made of porcelain: so elegant and dainty, and so thin-skinned. We had to be careful to make sure she didn't hurt herself when she exploded, because she was so impulsive. She would open her eyes wide, squeeze her mouth shut, put her ears back, and tighten her neck while fending off imaginary hornets with her tail. Moments like this made it difficult to know whether she was bluffing or would really explode.

Success at the upper levels is the direct result of successful communication.

Such behavior was impressive. And it left an impression on everyone around her, including other horses and her owner; it induced fear. Violetta made anyone around her tense, nervous, and reactive. Her young owner would not blink, her jaw would clench, her muscles would clench, and she would stop breathing every time Violetta jerked her head away from her. This anticipatory defensiveness caused long-lasting fear.

The interplay between feelings, differing interpretations of a situation, misunderstandings, and even the smallest human error can have a lasting impact on an animal.

Listening

Being able to work with this beautiful, jumpy mare every day was crucial, because that way I had time to listen to her. Some things went very smoothly; other things did not. Everything that had to do with her head was associated with tension, so I decided to avoid her head as best as I could and paid attention to the rest of her body. Our first session was in her stall and associated with lots of treats and rewards. It did not take long before she allowed herself to be handled. Soon she was happy to see me and would come to me without

We should always be open to hearing the horse's answer.

fear. Fewer and fewer treats were needed as she began to cheerfully accept praise.

I groomed her until she relaxed. I always had her bridle hanging over my shoulder, which, in the beginning, was enough to create tension. Even the attempt to try another bridle had the same effect. It seemed the issue wasn't the bridle itself, but approaching her and touching her mouth.

Violetta was clearly afraid. Because she was fearful, and making her owner afraid in turn, they were at an impasse. But it only took a few days before I could scratch her head. How did I make this happen? I showed no fear when she was reactive. Instead, I calmly continued what I was doing. I stayed close to her despite the fact that she was trying to chase me away. My goal was not to ride her, but first to reach her soul, her inner attitude.

Goal: Inner Attitude

After a few days of "reward school," I started to work on bridling her. Just placing the reins over her head caused her to completely freeze. But I continued with many pauses for scratches until she relaxed, because I wanted to change her inner attitude.

When I tried to put the bit in her mouth, she would clench her teeth. I didn't let this bother me; I had time. I just waited. It felt like an eternity before she was willing to open her mouth—but once she was, the reason for the misunderstanding soon revealed itself. As soon as I touched the noseband, her head flew up. I kept one hand on

Regardless of discipline or level, we need successful dialogue to build shared happiness.

the bridge of her nose, and didn't let go. It wasn't easy, but I waited until she started breathing again. As soon as I touched the buckles, her head would fly up again. As tempting as it was to rush or give up, I waited. She began to relax.

Eventually, I was able to buckle the noseband. As I put my finger under the buckle to avoid pinching her, the reason for her behavior became obvious. Clearly, at some point in her past, someone had tightened the buckle and pinched her skin, and intuitively, she had jerked up her head in a defensive gesture to try to move away from the feeling of pain. I would probably have reacted far more rudely than she had if someone had pulled my skin through a buckle. The next time someone approached her and tried to tighten her noseband, she reacted more strongly; her humans got

Trust is the quietest form of courage.

scared of her and perhaps even yelled at her, thinking she was badly behaved. Maybe they tried to calm her during these times and by doing so, had inadvertently reinforced her behavior—had taught her that jerking her head up would earn her pats and soothing, reassuring noises. Because nobody had figured out the actual cause of her behavior, they'd looked for quick answers: the reason was the tack, or a "naughty horse."

Violetta, on the other hand, associated human touch with pain, and learned that she could keep people at a distance with her defensive behavior. This behavior began to extend not only to buckling the noseband, but to bridling, then to anything touching her head, and ultimately to a human's arrival in the barn. This is what I call expectant or anticipatory defensiveness.

This mare was very smart and kind at her core. My hands stayed at her head regardless of how she reacted, and praise (page 33) was given out freely. My job was to convince this awesome horse that my hands weren't going to cause pain, and that she could enjoy being handled.

It took almost three weeks before I could bridle her without problems and without her sympathetic nervous system firing. After it worked with me, it also started to work with other employees. When her owner tried, her presence alone was, unfortunately, enough to restart the old pattern. Misunderstandings happen so easily and so fast, they are sometimes hard to identify; it takes time to understand and address the root causes. After some time, however, she was also able to safely and happily handle Violetta. We ended up training Violetta to the highest level, and her owner now takes her anywhere and everywhere. She set out on a journey to exchange misunderstanding for trust, and that path inevitably required real understanding and listening.

You can see in this one example how quickly trust can be destroyed. When we listen to our animals and pay attention to them, when we don't take mistakes personally but instead diligently search for the underlying causes, and when we give the horse the benefit of the doubt, then we can create happiness. That expectant behavior occurred several more times during the training of this wonderful horse, and not always defensively—for example, she believed that she knew exactly when I would ask for a lead change, and her ambition sometimes got in her own way. It was our job to keep her calm, to teach her patience, and to learn to listen to her.

This special horse, seemingly made of porcelain, with her unbridled work ethic, ambition, and "thin skin," taught us humans to be careful, thorough, and friendly. You can look forward to another encounter with her later in this book.

VIOLETTA

Team
Violetta, 8-year-old Westfalen mare. Here with us for dressage training.

Expressive behavior:
very tense; wide-open, unblinking eyes; squeezing her mouth shut; holding her head high; holding her breath; swishing her tail; pinning her ears

Purpose/communicative intent:
— defensive behavior
— aggression

Training path:
— develop behaviors to be rewarded
— work on her comfort zones and create a bond
— correct her internalized learning patterns
— understanding and communication

TRAINING IN HARMONY: OBJECTIVE OBSERVATION AND NON-JUDGMENTAL DIALOGUE

We must recognize that most problems—and often the biggest ones—in horse-human partnerships develop due to a failure to listen well enough and to misunderstandings.

Therefore, reading a horse's behavior should be the priority as you educate yourself. Reading means observing with all your senses, taking in all signals without judgment, and being open to the animal's answers. Reading means understanding the expressive behavior of the whole horse without judging his behaviors or anthropomorphizing them. Good reading is not defined by speed, but by thoroughness. Anyone can learn to be fully present with a horse carefully and mindfully.

Listening carefully to the horse means viewing him non-judgmentally and engaging all your senses.

Imagine sitting in a café and watching the people passing by. With a little distance, it's easy to observe them and notice their peculiarities—easier than with the person sitting with you at the table, and much easier than with yourself. The advanced study of "reading horses" is a very intensive course that requires a lot of homework, which includes observing him not only when he's interacting with you but also when he isn't.

READING HORSES

Sit with your horse in the paddock, in the pasture, and in the stable. Now watch. You are also welcome to keep a journal (you can find a sample of what this might look like on page 21).

While you study your horse in his free time, start at the front of his face, at the muzzle. How does his mouth move when he moves? What do his lips, tongue, and nostrils do? Watch him when he's eating, and when he isn't. Study his eyes: How often does he blink? How do his eyes look? What are his brows doing? Are they arched, pinched, or smooth and flat? How is the bulge above the eye (the soft tissue over the ocular ridge) shaped? Watch his ears: How mobile are they? Are they free of tension, actively listening, or passively resting? Is one ear doing something different from the other? How does your horse hold his head? Straight, at an angle, up, or down? What does his neck do? Is it relaxed, dropped, tight, raised, or lowered?

Look at his topline: is it relaxed, flexible, arched up, inverted, crooked, or loose? And his tail—is it mobile, active, tense, relaxed, pinched in, or perhaps even crooked or stretched? Do his legs move with relaxation and in rhythm in each gait, or are they stiff, tense, or out of rhythm? How are his hooves landing? Do they land flat on the ground or toe first? Observe his breathing, body temperature, muscle tension, and heart rate. Observe him with all your senses. Listen to whether he is holding his breath or breathing normally. Is he snorting, chewing, or grinding his teeth? Is he smacking his lips or rolling his tongue?

Look closely. Even closer! Film him with a slow-motion app and study what you see. Observe your horse without trying to interpret what he's doing. Keep a record and curb the impulse to put your own words in your horse's mouth.

Horses always read us humans perfectly.

READING HORSES: A STUDY GUIDE

Reading the horse means perceiving him from front to back, to recognize how he moves, how he uses space and time. It means being open to the horse's responses so as not to impose your own perceptions on him. This is the first and most important step in establishing a dialog based on trust.

We read the horse without judging it. The important points can be found in this overview. All these signals result in the expressive behavior of the horse. A single individual signal is not meaningful, only the totality of everything we perceive allows us to draw conclusions about the horse as a whole.

OBSERVING WITH EVERY SENSE

Maybe you'll catch yourself describing what you think the horse wants to say? If so, you didn't read so much as interpret: you actually revealed something about yourself, about what you think and what you want, instead of about your horse. A "true reading" only describes what is literally present, without embellishment or interpretation, objectively and factually.

HEARING WHAT ISN'T SAID

In interpersonal relationships, you know what to expect in a dialogue, what should be there and what shouldn't. Sometimes, we only notice later, when the situation is over, that something was missing. We remember, and then ask ourselves: Gosh, did he actually say "thank you"? Did he say hello to everyone here? Maybe there was a smile missing, or a nod that wasn't given. Hearing what isn't said—learning to pay attention to which signals are missing just as much as which signals are given—is a crucial aspect of learning to read horses.

READING WHAT ISN'T VISIBLE

If you observe your horse in his free time, you will notice how often he opens and closes his eyes. You will notice what his breathing is usually like and what he does with his tail. If you want to ride the same horse and stand next to him in the arena, then observe as you mount how frequently he blinks, what his breathing is like, and what his tail is doing. Do not think that everything is fine just because your horse is standing still. A horse standing still without blinking can be a ticking time bomb. If a horse is tense enough that he doesn't feel comfortable blinking, that could become a problem very fast. Recognize what is missing, not just what is there.

Did you know that horses greet people by blinking their eyes? It is sublime, quiet, and—once you have learned to recognize it—very touching. Horses greet other horses that walk past them with their bodies turned toward each other, gentle angles, softly raised ears, calm breathing, and—the most beautiful thing—blinking eyes.

Like a feather-light touch, they blink at each other and give each other their attention. Personally, I take it as a compliment when they make this gesture when I walk past them. And honestly, I've gotten into the habit of blinking back.

It's also important to notice what isn't there when you're riding. Riding as a physical dialogue means that I study the movement patterns and movement intentions of a horse both while he's in a relaxed state, in a safe environment, and while he's in tension and under physical and mental stress. Reading in these situations means more than just feeling or sensing while you're on the ground. When you feel or sense, do not think about your own feelings or about the things your horse might trigger in you.

Rather, just try to describe what you see.

"The true nature of another person lies not in what he reveals to you, but in what he cannot reveal to you."

—Khalil Gibran

☞ READING HORSES—OBSERVATIONAL JOURNAL

Head			
Position	low	high	in motion
Mouth	busy	quiet	chewing
Lips	relaxed	tight	
Tongue	quiet	licking	
Nostrils	wide open	tight	
Eyes	blinking	clear	bulging
Ears	forward	moving	pinned
Neck			
Position	low	high	
Muscles	relaxed	tense	
Tail			
Level	low	high	pinched
Position	straight	to one side	
Movement	quiet	active	swinging
Back			
Position	round/arched	down/inverted	
Flexibility	supple	stiff	
Legs			
Footfall	rhythmic	not rhythmic	
Landing of feet	toes/heels	flat	
Movement	calm	active	
Intention of Movement			
Energy	relaxed	tense	
Direction	to the inside	to the outside	
Sympathetic Nervous System			
Breathing	slow	fast	holding
Gut sounds	rare	occasional	often
Temperature	normal	high	low
Pulse	normal	slow	fast
Skin and Coat			
tension	relaxed	tense	
coat	smooth	raised hair	
Vocalizations			
	drawing in air	snorting	grunting
	squealing	whinnying	neighing
Managing Space			
Space	giving	demanding	
Position	facing forward	sideways	facing backward

Shared experiences and successes strengthen bonds within a team.

One example might look like this:

Independent forward movement; relaxed soft neck, relaxed active ears; longitudinal suppleness, swinging back and tail; relaxed muscles, even breathing, and tension-free skin. Relaxed, rhythmic movement.

This is the description of a typical worry-free horse, but we all know things will not always look this way. In the saddle, just as on the ground, we experience changes first with tension, and second spatially. Telling when the horse's look has changed, when his back has gotten tight or his muscles are tense, and so on, is similar under saddle and in-hand, but under saddle it's more direct.

LEARNING A FOREIGN LANGUAGE

Reading horses is a fantastic pastime. It's like learning a foreign language, although it's more primal—simple and direct. Rather than learning grammar and vocabulary, you're associating a "statement" directly with its behavioral origin. It's about space, dominance, affection, and security. It's about survival principles and clear boundaries. It's not about the type of emotion we cultivate, and it is not about the emotions the horse's behavior triggers in us, either. A horse always communicates clearly. He expresses an opinion and describes his current emotional state without worrying about potential consequences. A horse is always focused in the present, and communicates with body language and vocalizations. He speaks only one language, and is admirably honest about it.

If you want to become good at making your horse happy, you should put your own emotions, thoughts, and memories aside, and conduct a dialogue with your horse objectively in the here and now. This way, you have a good foundation for learning, and more importantly for understanding your horse's expressive behavior.

THE FUNCTIONAL PATTERNS

People tend to label animals. "He's just lazy," "He's always spooky," or, "He is so pushy, he can never wait," and so on. I'm sure you've heard this before, or perhaps even thought something like this about your own horse.

Three possible functional patterns are described here: The pushy horse may carry a lot of defensiveness within himself; the lazy one, passivity; and the scared one, an inclination toward flight. This is what it's all about: learning to read the expressive behavior of horses in a non-judgmental way and understanding that it's due to a corresponding functional pattern. Recognizing functional patterns should help you to draw objective conclusions.

A horse's behavior can generate strong emotions and produce misunderstandings in us humans. Our subjective perceptions can steer us in the wrong direction and destroy any chance of clear dialogue from the start. What we think an animal wants to express often doesn't coincide with what it's actually expressing.

Let's consider the spooky horse. A horse that is afraid pinches his tail, opens his eyes widely, does not blink, and has tension in his body and an elevated heart rate. When I interview people who describe their horses as being fearful, they frequently are unable to confirm any of these signals in their horses. Instead, they tell me their horses move off the path of travel, jump to the side, lay heavy on the bit, or rush away. I call this *pushing away*, which belongs to the push-pressure functional pattern group.

The "lazy" horse is a phlegmatic creature; he doesn't stress easily. I call this functional pattern *calm*, but it can also serve as a defense mechanism. To find out whether the horse's behavior is a defensive response or a functional pattern, you need to look at the whole horse and read all his signals correctly. This is very important, as your training approach will differ depending on which relevant functional patterns a horse expresses. The "lazy" horse can be motivated and made to work diligently with calm, clear driving aids and generous praise. However, a horse that shows defensive behavior by refusing to engage with questions or accept help is best approached in very small steps to strengthen the interrelational bond. In this case, it may be that the horse has an exaggerated sense of possible threats, causing an incorrect learning pattern.

By now you should see that reading the horse correctly is the be-all and end-all if we want to avoid misunderstandings. Let's move on to the six different functional patterns and their parts, which make up expressive behavior.

Praise incorporated into lessons guarantees success.

LIFE'S DRIVING FORCES

Pushing and pressuring are what drive life, without which nothing else can take place. Urges manifest themselves as hunger, thirst, curiosity, learning behavior, reproduction, playing, fighting, and much more. Described in terms of space, this is the willingness to leave one's own safe space to enter another's with initially unclear intentions.

The physical expression of this starts with movement. Whether it's with or without tension depends on the intent of the pushing. It can be a hostile demand, active harassment, or even an attack. Pay attention to how your horse might put pressure on you. Horses can be very aggressive, and they can display almost as much aggression as an attacking dog.

Horses can also be incredibly tender and gentle, even loving. The functional pattern of urging and pushing/harassing can be represented by a lack of boundaries in any direction, and you can probably see from my using the term "lack of boundaries" that this functional pattern needs spatial and emotional regulation in order to be safe for all parties involved.

Affectionate pushing-pressuring shows itself as closeness.

CALM

I see what I refer to as "calm" as a healthy degree of relaxation that can bring about deep inner peace. It's associated with the quiet blinking of the eyes, the soft, movable mouth, the relaxed ear and overall relaxed presentation of the horse's entire body, including steady breathing and calm movement.

On the other hand, sometimes a refusal to engage can look like calm, and it can be hard to see the difference. Any horse who evades certain demands placed upon him through passivity can be described as avoidant rather than genuinely relaxed. To be clear, in this case we're talking about a deliberate effort on the part of the horse to avoid work. You can identify this by assessing his overall behavior. Observe him in his free time. If he shows ambition and activity here, but appears unmotivated when it comes to clear and fair requests, his passivity is intended to avoid work.

However, there are also horses that have gotten stuck in a blockage, or have built up toxic tension. A horse like this may also appear calm, but as a rider, you can feel his back stiffen; you can feel when he is no longer in front of your driving aids, and his forward movement has lost its freedom. This functional behavioral pattern can also be identified by a lack of blinking, breath-holding, and increased muscle tension. Here, we can expect a potentially defensive response that must be approached with calm and caution. A horse that has a sympathetic nervous system response like this is actually in a highly alert state, and can deploy all his strength explosively in any direction—this horse isn't avoidant or calm, and needs a gentle guiding hand.

A horse won't voluntarily put himself in a situation that will force his sympathetic nervous system to sound the alarm. If this

Defensive behavior is part of every horse. It's helpful to recognize the early signals.

happens while you're working with your horse, you should carefully ascertain that the steps you're trying to take in training are small enough to make any given situation more manageable for the horse.

DEFENSIVENESS

Defensive behavior is a vital part of the behavioral repertoire of herd animals. Everyone has it, and everyone needs it. It ensures each horse has personal space in which to maneuver, and limits the space of the next horse over. Each animal manages his own space and maintains his own boundaries, and thus also the boundaries of his closest neighbor. This is the only way spatial communication among animals can work. And yet, if it gets out of hand, it can have very unpleasant consequences.

LINEAR OR COMPLEX?

Using the example of defensiveness, we can recognize and explain the difference between the linear and complex ways of thinking in humans and other animals. We can describe an animal's way of thinking as linear and a human's as complex.

Let's imagine you have to go to the dentist. You're pretty sure it won't be pleasant, but you remember that your last visit made your toothache go away. You can essentially plan for the future based on the past, and in doing so, you are able to emotionally fortify yourself against an unpleasant procedure. A horse can't do that. When the vet comes, your horse may experience an uncomfortable procedure or unpleasant treatment. An animal can't understand that this discomfort happened to him for his own good. This doesn't mean the horse isn't smart; he just understands time differently. The present

Rearing can be part of a defensive response...

...and cause this expressive response behavior in the horse.

moment is what matters to him, and a negative experience happening right now is enough to generate defensive behavior in his sympathetic nervous system.

This can present itself as a direct defensive response or, over the course of multiple experiences, as expectant defensive behavior. Any unfavorable learning experience can generate defensive behavior, which can become ritualized in no time.

With expectant defensive behavior in place, the horse might react as soon as the vet's car comes rolling into the barn yard. The animal's linear thinking means that we must create a positive learning experience in the present, even if we ask unpleasant questions of him. Some people would rather not ask unpleasant questions and try to avoid defensive behavior that way, but this isn't a sustainable or helpful approach. It's important for our horses to learn to trust us, and we can only achieve this if their learning experiences are positive ones despite the pressures, stressors, and adversities that life brings.

We humans must confront this defensive behavior again and again, outsmart it, and replace it. We rarely get past it. Putting on a halter for the first time, leading for the first time, lifting a hoof for the first time... these situations address defensiveness in its purest form. A horse isn't necessarily comfortable with what we humans want from him right from the start. There's both basic trust and basic mistrust (page 84) within a newborn foal, because both are absolutely necessary for a horse's survival. This is where you can establish yourself as a good trainer, because it's not the speed with which you silence defensive behavior that furthers training, but the sensitivity with which you convince the horse to agree to your requests. Identify defensive behavior in your horse as you prepare him for training. Check every move you make, every tool, and every question for possible resistance, and work through problems thoroughly, calmly, and kindly.

Ask your questions in a relaxed learning atmosphere and hand out plenty of praise. Don't ignore defensive behavior, but don't become defensive yourself because you're anticipating it; deal with it as it arises. Listen carefully to your horse as you work out issues in the moment. If you ignore defensive behavior, it can begin to snowball. It can also become expectant, and thus stifle dialogue before it even starts. At worst, it can silence the animal completely and cause him to turn inward and shut down mentally.

EXPRESSIVE DEFENSIVE BEHAVIOR

Clear expressive defensiveness always comes with tension in the whole body. Described spatially (see page 53), the horse will face forward while keeping his distance; his head is held high, his ears are pricked forward, his eye is worried and unblinking, his lips are pressed together, his nostrils are narrowed, and he holds his breath. His neck is tight and stiff, and his back is tense. His tail can be either tightly clamped or actively swishing. He might stomp, paw, dance around, or threaten to kick. The entire body of the horse appears tense and his breathing is shallow.

We should pay close attention to defensive behavior in our general dealings with horses. In this book, I give a lot of attention to defensive behavior, because it takes up a lot of space in our lives with horses. It is an important indicator of mistakes made in training, and the better we identify and process these mistakes, the greater our shared happiness will be.

SUBMISSION

This functional behavioral pattern can be de-escalating and calming, and can create harmony. We see submissive behavior in young horses often and clearly, with an obvious giving of space, and demonstrations of affection with elaborate chewing movements and infantile facial expressions. With his relaxed body and active gestures, he appears as submissive as, for example, a dog that slowly ducks down and presents its underbelly. This behavior is a crucial part of the behavioral repertoire of a species organized in groups, herds, and families, because it's the behavior of the peacemaker or mediator of disputes.

The expressive behavior is always spatially expressed with the body positioned sideways, with soft, blinking eye contact, a mobile ear and neck, and a relaxed overall appearance.

FLIGHT

Decisively leaving a place as quickly as possible to get to safety is escape behavior. It is a vital instinct that every one of us should have within us, and of course every horse should too. Flight behavior is a necessary instinct for survival, but should only be seen as an option when there is truly danger.

Submissive behavior defuses the situation immediately.

Offering soft, engaged body language toward the trainer.

When a huge barn door fell over while I was walking through it with my Westphalian gelding Berti, we both reflexively fled. What was touching was that he immediately ran to me to seek protection. It gave me a warm feeling to know that he saw me as his safe place, and that helped us both overcome the shock. It was a good thing that we both had a well-developed flight reflex, and even better that we had trust in each other that helped us recover quickly from the fright.

Expressive behavior in a flight pattern is demonstrated with wide open eyes that are unblinking, the corners of the mouth pulled back, strongly dilated nostrils, a head carried high, a clenched tail, a massively tense body, and a nervous system that is on high alert. When it comes to spatial language, the body is obviously turned away from the stressor. With this definition in mind, you can see that a horse that jumps away from a corner in the arena may not necessarily be in flight mode. You can find out whether you need to calm or regulate your horse by looking at his expressive behavior.

ACTIVE ENGAGEMENT

When a horse makes an active offer to engage, it feels like a compliment that the horse gives to his human. His body is upright and turned somewhat sideways, toward the recipient of his engagement, with a positive, open, blinking eye, and a moving ear. His mouth is soft and active, and his breathing is relaxed. A horse who actively engages is a joy to work with.

This is fertile ground for a deep and trusting bond.

The approachable, genuinely interested horse is good-natured, internally relaxed, and soft, self-confident, and polite. He's a thinking horse who's happy to answer questions, strives to find the right solution, and is motivated to work together with and take care of his human.

Such a horse either has a lot of "will to please," hence the functional behavior of active engagement, or has been so well trained that he can get through life well with genuine friendliness.

CHARACTER AND LEARNING PATTERNS

In this book, you will learn how you can change functional behavioral patterns and build happiness for both horses and humans. A large part of your work will be devoted to bonding, and some may be devoted to correcting learning patterns and inner attitude. Functional behavioral patterns are reinforced or changed through learning experiences the horse has over the course of his life. Although a horse's breeder plays a role when it comes to the genetic contribution to a horse's character, we, as our horse's guardians, coaches, and partners, have a great responsibility in shaping their learning patterns and structuring their inner attitudes. In order to begin to work with objectivity in dialogue with your horse, knowledge of the functional behavioral groups I've just outlined for you helps immensely. In this way, you can avoid bringing your own emotions into your interpretation of the expressive behavior of your horse, and can instead objectively describe the signals he's sending.

This is an important step toward allowing your partner in dialogue to have his own reality and his own feelings, and to express them to you. It is also a crucial step toward exchanging misunderstanding for understanding.

THE TOOLS FOR TRAINING IN HARMONY

In my system, just like in every other trade, it's incredibly important that the tools needed are used correctly and safely throughout the entire training process. Everything we want to achieve later can only be achieved if the foundation is good. I like to describe it as a house built on four pillars. If these pillars are stable, then the house I build on them could be a villa or even a castle. If the pillars are weak or uneven, maybe even wobbly, then they can't support anything but a tent. Decide where you want to live with your horse.

In the following pages, I'll introduce you to each tool, and discuss its meaning, use, development, and possible difficulties. Throughout the training process, the tools will reinforce each other. Therefore, they develop equally as training progresses.

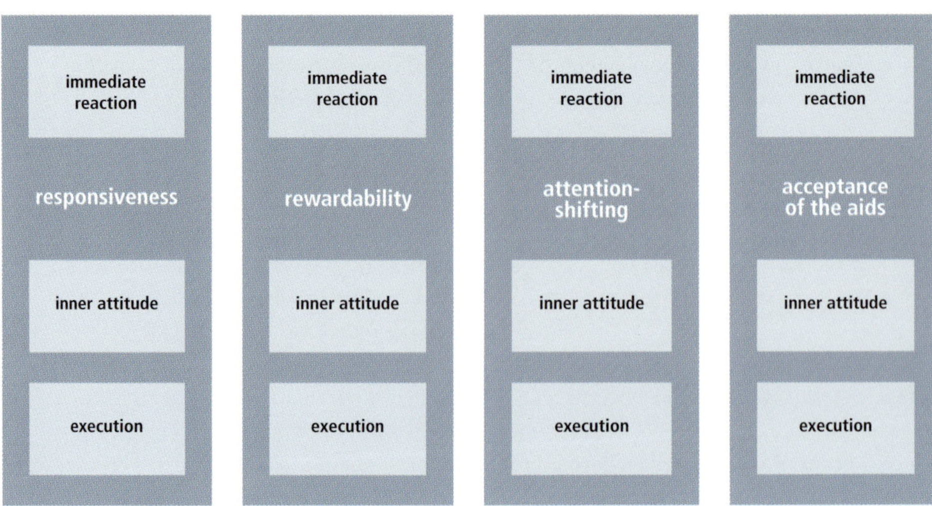

My system offers a stable and coherent foundation no matter the discipline.

An attentive horse will listen to you.

The dialogue should be light and friendly.

RESPONSIVENESS

WHAT IS IT?

The animal's name is like a public phone number: if you dial this number, the horse should answer and be ready to talk. But this also means that when you say your horse's name, you want to get his attention; you aren't saying it for no reason. This is similar to the use of interpersonal space. When I speak to someone, I expect to be met with mindfulness, politeness, and attentiveness.

WHY DO WE NEED IT?

Responsiveness is needed to orient the horse spatially and emotionally, to call him to us, and to ask him to focus on us. We need it when we work with him at liberty, to get his attention when leading, and when we ride him, to minimize outside distractions by asking him to focus on his "internal" environment—how he should move his body in response to our aids. This kind of responsiveness is like your horse's private cell phone number. If *that* number works well, your horse will always answer: no dropped calls and no dead batteries. When responsiveness is there, it's a truly rewarding feeling.

HOW IS IT TAUGHT?

First of all, we need to learn to only call the horse's name if we really want to make contact with him. Then we begin training in a low-stimulus environment that is familiar to the horse—for example, in the paddock, the stall, or the grooming station. The horse is haltered and his trainer stands at his shoulder, facing the horse. Now say the horse's name quietly and in a friendly manner. At this point, there are two options:

1. The horse reacts. He turns one ear toward you and focuses his eye on you. Praise him and give him a pat (see page 33).
2. The horse doesn't react. This doesn't mean he's being "bad." Maybe he doesn't even know what his name is yet, or what he's supposed to do. Then we start with attention-shifting (page 36). The moment the horse notices us, we say his name again, quietly and in a friendly manner, and we praise him.

As you have more success, the amount of stimulus around the horse can be slowly increased. We can start to work with the horse in more active and distracting surroundings, but he should still respond to his name.

HOW TO HANDLE PROBLEMS

When it comes to making mistakes with this exercise, there are plenty of possibilities. We can be impatient; we can fail to notice stimuli that are distracting the horse; or we can mess up our implementation of the traffic light principle, which I'll explain here. Imagine a traffic light as having four phases:

1. Green: saying the horse's name in a friendly manner, relaxed and attentive.
2. Yellow: a signal that shifts attention (page 36).
3. Red: activity, for example building tension, such as shaking a rope or tapping your jacket.
4. Green: the fourth phase is green again, because we want to return to harmony—and that is the friendly repetition of the horse's name, which we can also consider a form of praise.

If I do not get the horse's attention, I need to check whether the level of external stimulus is too high and also whether the horse has a real grasp of the lesson thus far. In most cases, it makes sense to repeat the exercise in a quieter environment. If the horse's response is insufficient here too, then I have overtaxed the horse, and I need to return to earlier parts of the training.

THE "POCKET DIAL"

Ever had this happen? Someone accidentally dials your number, and when you pick up, all you hear is the rustling of a jacket pocket or a muffled conversation that has nothing to do with you. If this happens more than a couple times, then you probably stop taking calls from this person, expecting more of the same. This is exactly what happens to many animals, because many people say an animal's name but have no expectation of any kind of reaction. So the horse may hear his name, but assume it means nothing, because that's what he's learned it means. To avoid this, people should hold themselves to the same standard they want to hold their horses to, and not dial the number if they aren't ready to talk.

Getting the horse to look at you by calling his name...

...can be a fun exercise.

When trust and respect are both part of training in harmony, the horse happily accepts praise.

REWARDABILITY

WHAT IS IT?

Rewardability refers to both the horse's acceptance of praise and the human's ability to reward him correctly. Essentially, high praise should produce clear, relaxed feedback from the horse.

WHY DO WE NEED IT?

I want to point out to my horse what he has done well and when he has found the right solution. He deserves praise for even trying to find the right answer. I need a horse that is receptive to praise in order to offer him comfort and mark success, and above all to give him the feeling of home, because then I activate his attachment system. In my opinion, praise is generally the most important tool in training, and I find that most of the time, this work is done far too superficially.

HOW IS IT TAUGHT?

Here, too, we look for a quiet, safe environment and halter the horse. Then we search for his favorite scratching spots. When we find one, his feedback should clearly indicate inner relaxation as shown by the lengthening of his upper lip, blinking of his eyes, relaxed and moving ears, and stretching of his neck, as well as lifting of his tail. Until this happens, keep looking for his favorite spots.

> *"To get the full value of a joy, you must have somebody to divide it with."*
>
> *—Mark Twain*

Take your time praising your horse; that time intensifies its effects and strengthens the bond between you.

Trust isn't taught so you can win prizes; it is the foundation of everything we teach.

This is attachment training. If it doesn't work right from the start, then your relationship may need a little more work and time to develop. The more you pay attention to rewardability, the deeper your relationship with your horse becomes, the more he's able to accept constructive criticism, and the more resilient and stable your whole training system becomes.

HOW TO HANDLE PROBLEMS

People often tell me, "My horse doesn't like that." I always ask: "May I?" Horses often back away at first; they may be obviously tense, and sometimes try to avoid the situation entirely by moving away with their whole body. Planning to take my time, I position the horse beside a wall, stay in the same spot at the horse's shoulder, and start patting him—almost massaging. The less he pushes away and the more he relaxes, the stronger my touch becomes. All the while, I observe his eye, the blinking of his eyelids, his mouth (whether it moves), his ear (whether it relaxes), and his breathing (whether it is deep and regular). This can take some time. I always wait for the moment when the horse becomes soft and begins to relax, no longer showing defensive behavior and maybe beginning to show trust.

When this happens, I lead the horse a few steps forward, stop again, and start all over. Praise until the praise works! Yes, this might mean there's no time to actually ride this horse that day, but we practiced something much more important: the tool that is the key to shared happiness.

What do I do if my horse is distracted during this exercise and doesn't even notice me?

Make sure the space you're working in is as free from excess stimuli as possible. A horse that has not yet learned to view people as a comfort may sometimes not be able to engage in this type of social grooming behavior. Every external stimulus becomes important. It may take time, but don't give up training rewardability. It's a crucial first step to furthering the rest of your horse's training.

What do I do if my horse doesn't want to be touched on part of his body?

This isn't a problem as long as it isn't expectant defensive behavior (see page 26). If the horse just evades your touch or tenses up, then look for a body part to scratch that makes it easier for the horse to let you in, and proceed from there.

What do I do if my horse threatens, bites, or kicks out?

If a horse's bond with humans has been broken to the point where he responds to a simple touch with an attack, then make sure he is safely tied or in cross-ties. Safely position yourself—for example, at his shoulder. Next, start feeding him treats like apples or carrots, because food also strengthens bonding. At the same time, scratch his withers and start massaging his crest. Only approach his back or head with your hands when he allows it. It's crucial to continue with this work until the horse is no longer defensive and has calmed down, because this is the only way he will understand that defensiveness is not the right solution. So make sure you have plenty of time to spend on this before you begin.

The search for the favorite scratching spot...

...is a conversation.

ATTENTION-SHIFTING

WHAT IS IT?

Wake up, interrupt, and focus your horse's attention. A cluck, a tap, or a slight tension in the upper body can shift the horse's attention. Praise, a sound, a word... any external stimulus can be included in this category. When riding, changing (sometimes losing) balance is a significant shift in attention. When we talk about attention-shifting, we are referring to the horse's ability to remain calm when his thinking or his current actions are interrupted and he has to shift his attention to something new. When riding, we call this "throughness."

WHY DO WE NEED IT?

Attention-shifting lays the foundation for throughness. It is the ability to guide the horse, first spatially, then physically, and later also acoustically (see "Clear, Simple Language" on page 70). For example, I can use attention-shifting to sharpen up my horse's responses. Interrupting the horse's focus to shift his attention requires respect—he has to consider you more important than any given external stimulus. Well-trained attention-shifting creates acceptance of the aids and helps avoid loss of control. It's like having well-understood ground rules prior to a conversation or argument, ensuring trust based on mutual respect.

HOW IS IT TAUGHT?

Like all other tools, we teach attention-shifting in a safe, quiet environment. The most important thing is inner peace and a generally kind attitude toward the horse. I want to ensure that the yellow phase of my traffic light is enough and I don't have to touch the horse at all. To do this, I must be focused and carefully follow my traffic light system, using two different signals, Plan A and Plan B (you can choose other words, phrases, or sounds for your Plan A and Plan B):

PLAN A: "With me." I say this to announce physical contact—for example, if I want to use the whip to encourage the horse to move his hind legs, or if I want him to lift his front leg during a Spanish walk. Likewise, I can use "with me" before placing my hand at the horse's poll to ask him to lower his head, or before I touch his cannon bone to ask him to lift his hoof. "With me" means something like "pay attention, I am about to touch you." It prepares the horse so he isn't startled when he is touched, but rather learns to expect it and prepares to react.

PLAN B: "Hey, hey, hey." This attention-shifting signal, spoken melodiously, is mainly used in free work; it means something like: "Be careful, you are on the wrong track. Please make me an active offer and pay attention to me." It is an announcement that in the next moment something will have to stop. This call to shift attention, different from Plan A, helps the horse focus—at least if we internalize this process and use it consistently.

I stand next to the haltered horse, holding the lead rope. Within the context of what I am doing, I repeat my attention-shifting signal the moment the horse isn't attentively focused on me. I increase my body's tension and start to communicate a bit more strongly—only as much as I need for the horse to notice me. Once I have his attention, I immediately relax my body and create harmony by giving the horse space and praising him for his response to my question.

If the horse doesn't respond to my first attempt to communicate...

...I wake him up...

...and once he's shifted his attention to me and our dialogue, I praise him with my voice.

I train this process without the horse having to make a mistake. It is not about punishment or intimidation; it's about the horse learning to stop a stimulus by shifting his attention. And the more quickly he responds, the more quickly he finds himself back in a loving comfort zone. I always use the touch-related "with me" (Plan A) when I plan to touch the horse to make a request, such as every time I ask him to lift his feet or yield in the barn aisle, or when I'm planning to touch him with the whip.

HOW TO HANDLE PROBLEMS

What do I do when my horse doesn't react correctly to my attention-shifting stimulus?

Create a calm environment and check your own mood. Make sure you're relaxed. Try to figure out what stimuli your horse has reacted to in the past; maybe you need an extra stimulus like increasing the tension in your body, stomping on the ground, moving the lead rope, swishing a plastic bag, slapping your hands on your jacket, or touching him with the whip. If you can warn him ahead of time that this extra stimulus is coming—signaling to him to say, "Heads up, I am going to stomp next!"—the horse can have an appropriate response, and a fair chance of stopping the extra stimulus before it appears. Do you remember the beautiful mare Violetta, who did not want to accept a bridle because someone had pinched her with it (page 15)? This was an expectant defensive behavior: Violetta wasn't reacting to the stimulus of the bridle itself, but to the cues leading up to that stimulus, trying to prevent it from happening to her at all. And she succeeded with her strong reaction. When I teach attention-shifting, I use exactly this learning process: the horse can make my extra stimulus stop, or prevent it from occurring, by giving me the correct response to my initial signal.

Subtle dialogue includes yielding space...

...as well as asking for space.

Simply put, this means that the horse learns that if he responds immediately to the "hey, hey, hey," no increased tension will be created, and I won't use any additional stimulus. In the best-case scenario, the extra stimulus should not involve physical contact.

What do I do when the horse positions himself right in front of me when I ask him to shift attention?
Reposition yourself at his shoulder and shorten the lead rope. I avoid being right in front of a horse as often as possible (see "Spatial Language," page 53). As soon as the horse accepts this position, relax your body language and praise him.

What do I do if my horse walks backward when I ask him to shift attention?
Stay close to his shoulder, move sideways and backward with him, and then move him forward. Basically, I hold my physical position in relation to the horse. Once forward movement is established again, give lots of praise until you see the horse accept his reward.

ACCEPTANCE OF THE AIDS

Accepting the aids is accepting boundaries in space and time. Every individual in a herd needs to both establish and accept boundaries. Boundaries are the basis of spatial language. Like all other tools, we practice this in context. Recognizing space, holding space, yielding space, and requesting space mean thinking and communicating spatially. It's done consciously and in a friendly manner, corresponding to the natural law of this kind of language—it is training in harmony.

WHAT IS IT?

A well-trained horse is able to respond to a human's request for space in a straightforward and easy way. He gives the requested space while staying relaxed and calm, without becoming overly submissive or unstable. He will voluntarily yield the space, as if participating in a conversation with a counterpart rather than submitting to a ruler.

WHY DO WE NEED IT?

We need to establish boundaries to define how we dance with each other, to stay on track or get on track, to create mutual understanding and regulate space peacefully, and to establish a pecking order. I need boundaries every time I physically interact with a horse; it's the basis for groundwork, leading, liberty work, and preparation for working under saddle. This spatial language gives the horse direction and leads to an agreement between horse and human based on the natural laws of spatial language.

HOW IS IT TAUGHT?

When being led, a horse should learn to give his handler space when asked. To teach him this, position yourself at the horse's shoulder and hold the lead rope in the hand closest to the horse. Turn your outside shoulder toward the horse with your sternum facing the horse's shoulder joint. Your outside hand holds the whip. The verbal command is, "Walk on," basically asking for forward momentum. You want your feet to land in the footsteps of the horse's front hooves, and the horse's movement will be backward and sideways. If the horse does not yield, I will say, "With me," in a friendly, calm way, and give a light touch on the atlas (first cervical vertebra) for as long and as intensely as needed—using the handle of the whip, and taking care not to frighten the horse—until the horse is ready to yield. Then I repeat, in a calm and quiet voice, "Walk on." I stop asking for space after just one step, and I will praise extensively. The smaller the steps, the friendlier the tone, and the more clearly I teach it, the more quickly it will be understood; asking for space shouldn't make a horse feel threatened, it should just call his attention. What is important here is that you as the handler don't attack the horse and don't try to get too close to him. The horse should establish a good distance and allow himself to be spatially regulated—which means you should not only be able to ask for space, but also turn the horse and direct him.

Calmly but unequivocally, we should be able to ask for...

...both space and direction.

HOW TO HANDLE PROBLEMS

What do I do if my horse tries to stand right in front of me when I ask this question?
Correct your intention to move more clearly into the shoulder and stay there within the movement. Maintain your existing space—keep your position relative to the horse the same. This ensures the horse cannot get you out of this position and will not end up in front of you.

What do I do if my horse tries to evade backward and refuses to yield sideways?
Increase the intensity of your intention to move toward the horse, and work significantly more slowly.

What do I do if my horse will not move at all?
You may have to increase the degree of stimulus with the handle of your whip on the atlas (C1) for a brief amount of time, until the horse decides to move away at least a little bit. Immediately praise him prior to asking again.

Conflicts are quickly exacerbated by mutually threatening behavior.

What should I do if my horse turns around his own axis, but without moving his hind legs, so he ends up pushing me away a little with his shoulder?
Shorten the lead rope and prevent the horse from moving forward with that hand ("close the front door"). If the horse takes even one step backward or sideways, stop the exercise and praise him.

You can probably see by now that less is often more, that calmness and friendliness should set the tone when dealing with the horse, and that any form of escalation should be avoided. Horses do things that horses do, including sometimes not yielding the space they are being asked to give.

Stay positive but remain firm. If it makes sense, insist on the correct answer; if it makes sense, give in. It is the combination of willingness to insist and willingness to compromise that makes for a good leadership style.

THE THREE CHARACTERISTICS OF THE HORSE'S RESPONSE

Prompt, affectionate, and correct—this is how every answer to your questions should come across at the end of training. And these answers should come from a motivated, happy, and relaxed partner. This is how I rank and describe these three elements:

1. **Prompt:** We need an immediate reaction every time in order to enter into a real dialogue with our horse. An ideal response could also be described as quick, unhesitating, or in front of the driving aids. Whatever you want to call it, when you dial your horse's phone number, you shouldn't be put on hold, or stuck listening to it ring a hundred times, or have to call more than once to get an answer.

Speak quietly, because he is listening to you.

2. **Friendly:** Kindness goes a long way. This statement applies to both participants in the conversation. And just as I teach people to ask friendly questions, using slow, small steps, we also need to train horses to give friendly answers—to have a good inner attitude. Developing a good inner attitude in the horse is certainly one of the tasks of the trainer and coach, but so is asking careful, friendly questions. You get out what you put in. The horse's understanding, honesty, and sensitivity shouldn't be greeted with a harsh, negative tone from his trainer. He should be treated gently and guided clearly.

3. **Correct:** In the end, the horse should do everything right: correctly, perfectly, completely. This is the aspect that seems the most important to many people. But the purpose of dressage, its true meaning, isn't training for the circus, or exercising at liberty. It isn't even riding. I'm convinced that dressage is about communicating. The correctness of the answer should never be considered more important than its promptness, or the degree of gladness with which it's offered. Promptness and friendliness are much more important, because as long as your horse is "tuned in," attentive, and happy to be working with you, you can ask him your question as many times as you need to in order to get the right answer. If someone listens to me, then I can help them, I can work as a team with them, and that is what it's all about. Do you want to work as a team with your horse, no matter the discipline? Do you want to understand each other, trust each other, have fun, and be successful? Then you have to first be open, listen to each other, trust each other, and build a bond, and only then can you start learning together.

It was my language arts teacher who taught me this. In his class, we often had to learn poems by heart and then recite them. I usually remembered the first verse quite well, but then the words just stopped and I remembered nothing else, even though I had always studied thoroughly. When my teacher noticed, in a testing situation, that I was suffering this sort of "blackout," he quietly said the first two or three words of the next verse. Just like that, I got back on track, and my recitation was a success. In that moment, he showed me I could trust him and myself, and gave me the confidence that comes from succeeding at a difficult task.

The three characteristics we want in a response also apply to how we ask the question. If you are attentive, "tuned in," and committed, then you can help your equine partner find the right solution. This is how my system works. I am deeply grateful to my language arts teacher for the lessons in empathy he shared with me.

EVERYTHING TOGETHER

Now we're going to combine these three characteristics with our four tools.

With the tool of **responsiveness**, combining it with each element sounds something like this: The horse is immediately approachable and friendly, and can be put in the right position.

This means that my horse can always be clearly oriented with ease, and not only that: while I can orient him spatially and emotionally, he also politely and attentively offers me a few responses. It feels like I could walk on clouds.

Combined with **attention-shifting**, describing the three elements of the horse's response might look something like this: My horse doesn't react to his name, no problem. I say quietly, "Hey, hey, hey," and he looks at me, turns to me, and focuses on me, waiting for further information. What a powerful feeling. One word and I can simply stop and turn this wonderful, strong animal—without hurting his feelings, without forcing him into a corner, without humiliating him or pushing him into tension. The immediacy of his attention-shifting demonstrates that he's attentive and willing even though he didn't react to his name the way I wanted him to. And now that he is listening to me, I can tell him what I would like; in this case, I'll reward him for his correct inner attitude, demonstrated by his attention-shifting.

The three characteristics in the context of **rewardability** might look like this: You scratch your horse's neck in a highly stimulating or unfamiliar situation, and he drops his head even then. He fully engages with you due to the previous training involving his comfort zones, which works immediately and strengthens the bond between you. The way your horse puts himself completely in your hands despite environmental stressors is truly a great compliment to you and your work establishing a solid bond. Moments like this will give you the wonderful feeling that you are your horse's person: his safe space and his home. If you find that this isn't yet the case for you and your horse, don't despair, but instead continue to work on bonding with him; work on his ability to accept rewards and praise, until his expressive behavior matches the way you ask your questions.

Once the horse has learned to listen...

...he can be directed clearly by name...

... and he is easy to reach at liberty.

If we look at the three characteristics within the framework of **acceptance of the aids**, then the following is the correct reaction: Being able to regulate space and time with ease and without resistance, combined with the feeling that my horse respects my individual space without any problems and remains relaxed while respecting my boundaries, not only allows me to gain confidence but also keeps me physically safe. After all, there are approximately 1,200 pounds of horse playing with 150 pounds of human—but if everyone sticks to the rules, playing is fun.

Have you ever played with your horse? Playing—which can be an important element of bonding between individuals of any species—is often neglected in human interactions. Sometimes, playful behavior is characterized by competition for dominance, and sometimes by a violation of personal space. Neither one of these options is fun, though. So if we do play with our horses, then it makes sense to play with an awareness that we are physically inferior, which means something like this: I give space and I let my "opponent" "win." Nevertheless, there are rules. It's not about letting your horse chase you around randomly, but rather cleverly dodging away, outsmarting each other, and then getting "caught" in the end. As long as the rules of engagement are well explained, it's fun and joyful for our horses to share in play with us. Maybe this is a good idea for you: After training, just get off the horse and have some fun with your four-legged partner.

If you want to try to motivate your horse to play, most likely nothing will happen at first. Try to keep him focused on you and give him space again and again; dodge him, and if he chases you, then praise him extensively. Playful behavior can be developed particularly well in a round pen. Try to turn your horse again and again (see "Working at Liberty," page 164) and give him space. This alone is enough to prompt playful behavior in most horses and kick off a desire to pursue their partner. And when your horse has "got you," celebrate him, find his favorite scratching spot, and, using social grooming, teach him that this is behavior you will reward.

Some horses need a few days to buy into the offer to play, and others do it immediately. Use play to create a bond between you and your horse; develop it carefully and systematically. This work will help you successfully bond with each other, and it will create strong rewardability in your horse and happiness for both of you.

For all of this, we need complete understanding and respect for boundaries—the horse must promptly make room when I need it, and give me space in a friendly, relaxed manner. This may sound difficult, but my system trains exactly this, and does it logically, holistically, in a friendly way that aligns with the natural laws of the horse's non-verbal language.

TRAINING EMPLOYEES

You'll recall that I placed more emphasis on the first two of the three characteristics: the promptness of an answer, and giving it with a good inner attitude. We can always achieve the third characteristic, namely correct execution, when the animal is focused on us and happy to be with us. Much like the CEO of a company would like employees to be motivated, enthusiastic, loyal team players, not soldiers who blindly follow orders, it should be important to you that your horse is willing to respond to you, that he likes doing so, and that he respects you. If he does, all you have to do is show him the correct path. If you can achieve that, then you have graduated.

THE FIRST STEPS IN BUILDING HAPPINESS

How do you actually get started? The very first step is to set up your classroom: a quiet, low-stimulus environment with a safe outer boundary, such as a longeing area, a paddock, an outdoor riding ring, or an indoor riding arena with good solid footing. Find a quiet space with as few external distractions as possible for your teaching time. Then make sure you have the appropriate equipment: sturdy gloves, good shoes without spurs, a well-fastened and well-fitting halter with a good quality lead rope, and brush boots or tendon boots. You also need a whip that is about five feet long—and a ton of inner calm.

CREATING A BOND

It is rewardability which opens doors; rewards are the positive contact you start with that creates a good learning environment. And so, as a budding builder of happiness and harmony, start doing exactly that. Enter your classroom with your horse, and find his favorite scratching spots.

But what if my horse:

— won't stand still?
— constantly paws and is restless?
— bumps into me?
— bites or kicks me?
— throws his head?

Then you move these first steps into his stall, to the cross-ties in the aisle, or to his own paddock (without other horses), so you can make it possible for him to enjoy praise. Bonding (page 88) doesn't happen in one day. Relationships grow slowly and need lots of care. This is something you should focus particularly hard on as you work toward harmony.

When your horse begins to accept your touch with relaxation, maybe even with affection, then you can start to address his responsiveness. For me, since I have already become a person of comfort in my horse's life, I can move to his shoulder and say his name quietly and kindly. Now, as you already know, one of two things may happen:

1. My horse reacts with his ear and eye turned toward me.
2. My horse doesn't react at all.

If I get the first result, I immediately start praising him and doing things that bring him comfort, such as scratching. If I get the second result, I start to increase the stimulus for him by saying, "With me," in a quiet, friendly way, and if he still doesn't react, I increase my own body tension or give a small "half-halt" with the lead rope (or lightly shake the lead toward his head) until he pays attention. In that moment, I repeat his name and praise him enthusiastically. Now you can see how simple the use of these first three tools really is. You can practice this in a dry run with another person first.

Bonding happens when you create happy, relaxed moments together.

LOVING CONSISTENCY

If the exercises work smoothly, which can be the case after just a few training sessions, then you can gradually allow for more stimuli. Always pay attention to the three aspects of your horse's response, and be thorough and consistent. The more solidly this training is instilled, the faster you can move on to teaching other concepts, whatever you want your individual horse to learn. You should use the tools you have learned carefully. Develop this bonding system correctly so it will last, and develop this new way of communicating thoroughly, because this is the foundation on which all future lessons will be built.

☞ YOUR TRAINING DIARY

Set up a training logbook or a training diary to document your progress. This will help enormously to bring structure to your vision, your goal, your current state, and your questions and problems. It will also help you look in the rearview mirror; after a few weeks of training, you can reread it and see how far you've already come. This will be a resource to document training habits, new "vocabulary," and, above all, your successes. You'll find this diary invaluable as your training progresses, and it will provide a much-needed framework for you to help your horse succeed.

COMMUNICATION —*A Dialogue With the Horse*

E

A SYMPHONY OF MEANING

When communicating with animals, we should try to convey information by using the communication channels that animals employ.

Let's first look at three types of communication: spatial, physical, and acoustic. That list is written in the order in which horses process information. They use space easily. They can move into a space and "own it" incredibly quickly. They can recognize escape routes, calculate distances, and monitor what is happening around them closely. Not only do they have excellent spatial awareness, but they also convey important information through the way they use space. As herd animals, horses are experts in spatial language. They also use clear and distinguishing expressive behavior—body language—which we often refer to as gestures or facial expressions.

Riding as a successful dialogue means being in touch with your horse.

Acoustic language—communicating through sound—is limited in horses and is in no way comparable to human language. People communicate primarily through spoken language, which is to say we use acoustic representations (words) for feelings, memories, objects, noises, sensations, and so on. Usually when we use the word "speech," we're referring to this type of acoustic communication. While we use spoken language easily, and it can be complicated and extensive, our reliance on it makes it easy for us to lose sight of other means of communication. Physical communication, such as gestures and facial expressions, holds meaning for us, but with spatial communication, most people are at a complete loss.

A BREEDING GROUND FOR MISUNDERSTANDINGS

It is precisely this difference between human and horse prioritization of communication methods that can turn into a breeding ground for misunderstandings. We can expose, clarify, and, in the best-case scenario, completely avoid these misunderstandings if we are able to change the way we prioritize these methods of communication to match our horses' perspective. This can help us better understand and appreciate what they are trying to tell us at any given moment.

Be deliberate in using good communication habits when you are developing a dialogue with your horse on the ground.

Obviously, trusting relationships develop when we can better understand and be understood.

We need to truly grasp these three different methods of communication to give the horse the best possible support in his training. On the ground, horses understand spatial and body language best.

As riders, we use other signals that present themselves physically or bodily: the seat, leg, and rein aids, balance, and perhaps touches with a whip can all ultimately tell a horse what to do. But acoustic language remains the same whether we are on the ground or in the saddle, which means we can take our vocal cues with us. So it makes sense to deliberately train and use all three communication methods. It supports the horse and creates deep trust.

For you and your horse to be happy, you are responsible for working on yourself as well. Introducing a tidy, clear language you can use with your horse means maintaining communication habits that allow both you and your horse to be happy in this training space.

LEARNING FROM EXPERIENCE

Anja said she had been involved in dressage for a long time, but now only wanted to ride for pleasure. Next to this serious-looking woman stood her two-year-old pinto Quarter Horse, Johnboy, who she hoped to train herself. Except he wasn't really standing; he was fidgeting, almost stepping on her feet, throwing his head around and flicking his tail nervously.

Then he just pushed her. Every time he moved in her direction, she moved away. She made sure she didn't get hurt by giving space—but she didn't realize that she was communicating with her horse the whole time. She was constantly encouraging Johnboy to invade her space, because whenever he pushed her out of her space, she patted his neck reassuringly and said, "It's okay." But no, nothing was okay at all. With her behavior, Anja created a misunderstanding.

This could create toxicity within their relationship, which could last for the rest of this horse's life if it went unaddressed. He was begging her to regulate him, to be

The principles which guide the herd are direction, space, and regulation.

shown the spatial boundaries he should respect and his emotional direction. Many horses—all young horses, in fact—do this, because they have to test their limits.

Both demanding space and giving space...

Laws of Safety

Johnboy's behavior was based on the herd principle: spatial language, positioning and demarcation of each individual's safe space, and constant checking of boundaries are what give each individual security and protection. He was asking Anja what the laws of their herd were, the laws that governed his safety—and each time, Anja was unintentionally replying, "What rules? I don't know the rules." With her actions, Anja accidentally told the young gelding it was fine for him to invade her space. Every time she gave him more space, she believed she had to calm him down; but it was not him who was upset, it was her. Her calming words acted as positive reinforcement for an undesirable behavior. Johnboy wasn't receiving helpful answers to his questions from Anja. He couldn't understand her, and she in turn was stuck in old habits and didn't know how to understand his questions.

...are appropriate means of communication with herd animals.

Spatial language has nothing to do with constant driving pressure or with dominance behavior. It's the basis for peaceful coexistence within a group, herd, or pack; each member of the group is equal. It's an easy-to-learn, clear language.

Personal Space

The first step: we worked on keeping personal space and demanding personal space (page 38). Anja learned not to leave her position when her horse demanded it. It took real mental fortitude to overcome old habits.

Every time the pretty pinto pushed into her personal space, she said, "Back," and sent him away by moving into his space. It took a few repetitions before he became more careful, before the "back" was enough of a warning to keep him out of her personal space. After this first step was established, it was about demanding and giving space. Anja now steered her movement toward his front feet and demanded more space—or she steered away from him, let him walk around, and gave him space. She realized Johnboy was only assertive if he didn't understand or couldn't respect what she was requesting. We broke this dialogue down into smaller pieces, created more easily attainable goals, and got results more quickly. In this way, Anja learned to stand her ground and communicate her point of view in the clearest way possible, and to set the tone in a friendly but determined way.

The Pushy Horse

At first, Johnboy accepted this "comfort zone" training to a limited extent, but he quickly used it to become pushy again. He would threaten to bite on one side and demand space on the other. So, we defined a radius, like a hula hoop, around Anja, which Johnboy was not allowed to enter. He had to learn to respect her defined safe space. Interestingly, this physical distance can create a space for emotional closeness. It puts the human in a position to request space, and Anja learned to do this instead of giving way and unwittingly praising Johnboy for encroaching on her space. Johnboy soon understood what he was supposed to do and participated enthusiastically. I was happy to see more and more mouth activity like licking and chewing. He also began to lower his neck and head around Anja more frequently.

JOHNBOY AND ANJA

Team
Johnboy, two-year-old Quarter Horse gelding
Anja, former dressage rider

Expressive behavior:
Tossing his head, active body and tail, threatening eye, demanding space

Purpose/communicative intent:
— predominantly being pushy
— not respecting boundaries
— no particular orientation in any direction

Training path:
— properly recognize and correctly react to the horse's expressive behavior
— bring quiet and calm into training
— train attention-shifting
— improve responsiveness and rewardability
— organize space: keep your safe space, request space, give space, maintain focus and direction within the space, help the horse find security within his own space
— maintain relaxation and focus by creating a framework for training with a safe space with boundaries

Harmony develops when space is respected and communication is clear.

FINDING CLARITY

Horses are constantly communicating. They always read their human, and they always have a plan ready.

If you're not sure whether or not you're making a mistake like the one Anja made, then have someone take a video of you. Watch the video and notice the pace, attitude, and clarity of your own intention when you move. Assess your horse's responses. It's always easier to see from the outside—if you're in the middle of it, you sometimes don't notice small mistakes.

The channels of communication are fairly easy to manage. It bears repeating: the most important factor is how they're prioritized. This is where we need to shift our thinking to place spatial language first, followed by body language. We use these two to train the third: acoustic language, which—don't forget—we can take with us into the saddle. If we use these channels of communication correctly, then our horses can understand us, and out of understanding grows trust. That's the goal.

SPATIAL LANGUAGE

THE MAGIC OF THE HERD

In the course of earning my Master's degree in Animal Science, I was able to study the group interactions of many different species. Whether it's a herd of horses or a swarm of insects, I find observing these dynamics utterly fascinating. You may feel the same way when you see wild horses, the herds of zebras or gazelles in the Serengeti, or a flock of geese taking flight. By closely observing herd systems, I've learned to decipher the spatial language employed by animals, and now have a much better sense of the bigger picture.

The spatial language of animals is a synergy between dominance and a willingness to compromise. It equips each individual with their own place in the group. Everyone can defend their own boundary, and in turn accepts the parameters established by their herd mates. In this way, proximity and distance are easily regulated, even while under stress or when moving at top speed.

In the animal kingdom, dominance is not a one-way street, but a movable concept. A herd is an ever-changing construct geared to maximize survival, and it can't survive immutable rules. Too rigid a set of rules would destroy the unique system of bonding, respect, and trust that governs a herd. With this in mind, let's look at the horse's artful way of managing space.

"The whole is greater than the sum of its parts."
—Aristotle

In nature, the herd system is a structured, holistic, and successful survival mechanism.

SAFE OUTSIDE, ENGAGED INSIDE

One of the most valuable and intensive lessons of my life was learning how horses develop spatial language. My teacher was a four-year-old dressage mare who had just given birth to her first foal. The moment of birth was both thrilling and touching. Daily Pleasure, our mare, was very comfortable with us thanks to my work with attachment and bonding training. She seemed to be waiting for us, only starting the birthing process once we were all with her. We thought we would have to hide somewhere, but she came to me, pressed her head against my stomach, and invited me into this intimate moment. I'll go into this in more detail in the chapter on bonding (page 84).

Being able to participate in dialogue with our horses is pure happiness.

Immediately after the birth, we were impressed by how carefully Daily placed her huge hooves, and how well she organized the space of her very large stall; she was obviously 100 percent focused on her foal. The next day came their first outing. Daily had direct access from her stall to a paddock, which in turn opened into a very large pasture. Adjacent pastures held our geldings.

At first it seemed as if the foal—who we named Just Magic (Jupp)—was accompanying his dam, but we soon realized she was actually following him: Jupp determined the path, and Daily was there as his bodyguard. She surveyed the space around them, shielded his little body with hers, and pushed herself between him and the other horses. She dominated the space while only moderately influencing his direction, and only ever to keep him in a safe space. Jupp set the pace, and his dam never blocked his efforts to move forward. She didn't stop him; she protected him with her body, and she was his "external safety." There were two goals that she pursued with her foal: bonding and protection. Nothing else. She offered him what I call "home," a safe place. Showing him the boundaries of this home was Daily's first task.

I realized as I watched them that if I wanted to be "home" for my animals, I needed to be able to show them the boundaries of their home, and while they were inside it, I would need to provide pleasure, comfort, safety, and protection. I would have to learn spatial language, which gives them a "safe outside" and a bond within a focused, "engaged inside." Only then would I be able to achieve my goals with the animals.

A horse that is correctly on the aids feels a safe "outside" and a focused, engaged "inside" with the rider's help. This absence of negative tension creates throughness.

THE HORSE'S "HOME"

As riders, we encounter the combination of inside and outside—the diagonal aids—when we ride with the inside leg to the outside rein. In fact, these are the external aids we use to keep the horse on the desired path, influence his pace, and create his frame. The inside aids create activity, bending, and relaxation. The fact is, when a horse is trained this way, he lets go internally and is happy and on the aids. Here, it makes sense to carry the idea of inside and outside to its conclusion: the balanced rider who gives her horse a "safe outside" and an "engaged inside" can also be a home, or safe place, for the horse.

LIBERTY WORK

Even in liberty work, the main focus is to show the horse the path to "inside," to get his attention and to eventually get to the point where the "outside" becomes unimportant. If I simply let a young horse run free in the arena, he will organize the space to keep as much distance as possible between himself and me. He'll run along the outermost boundary of the riding arena, and the more pressure I put on him from the inside, the faster he'll run and the more reliably he'll keep his distance from me. When I want him to change direction, he'll usually turn outward—he'll turn his croup toward me, to the inside, and his head will point to the outside. In liberty work, however, I want the horse to turn inward, toward me, and not run toward that outer boundary. I want him to pay attention to me, on the inside. If I want to be a home for the horse in liberty work, I can do it through comfort zone training, responsiveness training, attention giving, and respecting boundaries. This is the only way a horse can learn to figure out the path I want him on. (I'll discuss this further starting on page 164.)

With her foal, my mare Daily dominated quietly, not rigidly, and she managed their space to keep Jupp safe. She followed and guided him, intending only to protect him with motherly care. The safe "outside" and the loving "inside" created a supportive bond. Seeing it work so well in nature motivated me to implement this system in every aspect of my training practices.

FINDING THE RIGHT PATH

Imagine a horse is standing at a crossroads and has three options: right, left, or straight ahead. How can he pick the right way to go? As I've mentioned, a horse can calculate escape routes, exits, or routes that lead to specific destinations at top speed. He can also calculate the space between him and a partner, and almost always knows exactly where his body is in relation to others. If a path has been successful before, the horse will choose it again. This creates a learning pattern.

If I work with a horse on the ground, my intention isn't to dominate him, but rather to practice possible solutions to the questions I will ask him. Let us consider the principle of asking for space: I want my horse to yield to me by walking backward and sideways when I walk toward his shoulder. Why shouldn't he just push his way forward and bolt, walk backward, or push against me? In the learning phase, my horse may offer each of these answers. And I should be able to close the door to each of these incorrect options and let him find the right solution, calmly and in small steps.

We repeat this exercise not to subjugate the horse, but to help him find the choice that solves the riddle. Horses that have previously learned to push or bolt have found what they see as solutions, but are actually incorrect learning patterns; they may repeat them over and over. The goal of successful training is to understand how to best manage the available space so the horse finds the right solution.

By calling his name and using unambiguous body language...

...I can give my horse clear spatial guidance...

...toward the answer I'm looking for.

TWO TO ONE IN THE HORSE'S FAVOR

Since the goal when giving space and tuning in is always for the horse to learn to focus on me and to choose to come inward rather than go outward, I always work with a give-to-request ratio of two to one. In other words, I give twice as much space as I ask for. I let the horse follow me—I yield space to him—and then I move away, asking for space for myself, and then I let him follow me again. Only with this ratio in place will I be able to remove the lead rope and work with my horse in this space. I will become my horse's home when his responsiveness and rewardability are well-established, when I can ask him to shift his attention, and when I can manage the space (acceptance of the aids). Notice that I'm relying on my four foundational tools.

THE SPACE AND THE TRACK

Let's jump ahead: Jupp is seven months old, a teenager who wants to be taught every day and needs answers to his questions about spatial language. To do this, he needs teachers, who should be loving, patient, and clear, and have plenty of time. For us, the foals are taught by our geldings and our pony stallion. Watching from the sidelines, this is like a masterclass. There are no brutal attacks that would endanger the health of the youngsters. They play, drive each other away, and snuggle. Then it starts all over again. The adult horses are checking Jupp's ability to yield space by positioning themselves close to his shoulder and asking him to yield repeatedly. They turn him in a particular direction, and then they give him space, letting him close the gap. This is followed by either a gentle nibble (social grooming) or a game of submission. In these games, the teachers can also yield to the youngster and make room for him, just as they have previously asked of him. Horses spend a great deal of time discussing space—keeping it, giving it, and asking for it. This spatial language means protection, security, and ultimately trust.

For the relationship between horse and human, this means we should learn to keep, give, and request space. The leading position is at the shoulder. From this position we can observe and interpret the heads and necks of our four-legged partner. We are in the driving position. At the beginning we need a safe "outside," like, for example, a wall. Initially, the direction of movement is simply straight ahead. Since we as humans are too stiff and slow, not to mention physically too weak to truly limit a horse's use of space, we use tools such as walls, halters, and ropes. Daily could do all this without any mechanical aids, because she's physically stronger than her foal.

Asking for space creates respect and trust.

☞ SPACE MANAGEMENT SCHOOL FOR HUMANS

When we humans pay attention to our own expressive behavior, we often find that we do not come across as clearly as we think we do. "Space management school" helps us reflect on our attitude and our effect on others. It helps us express ourselves more clearly to prevent misunderstandings, and it helps us understand how to improve our ability to send clear signals with our bodies.

The expressive behavior of humans should be soft, friendly, and relaxed. It's important to pay attention to your own gestures and facial expressions.

With the signal to "walk on," we ask the horse to move while holding our position at his shoulder with soft body language.

By turning toward us (which horses learn first from leading), we develop recall. Here, we hint at a turn and...

... ask the horse to position himself facing us. With a soft and inviting posture, we offer the horse a "landing place" and praise him extensively.

Horses mirror us. Therefore, it's important to pay attention to the image you project. An inviting presence produces an attentive horse.

When rewarding the horse, be authentic and truly honor him. Horses can sense authenticity, and they value it.

When this works reliably, we can increase the distance between us and the horse. As long as our communication is still clear, the answer will also still be clear to the horse.

"Praise until the praise works" should be your words to live by. This is how we can truly become a safe haven for our horses.

Jupp, a young horse full of energy, intelligence, and zest for life. He needs clear and gentle guidelines to grow up feeling safe and happy.

CHANGES IN SPATIAL BOUNDARIES

Jupp is full of questions. Pushing and questioning (page 24) is what drives him. All his questions are looking for the same basic information: he wants to know what he can do, what's allowed. Can he bite? Move into someone's space? Push them away? Eat that food? Get someone to cuddle with him? And so on. Outwardly, these questions look like he's being a pushy little guy. Remember Johnboy (page 49)? Such questions are always accompanied by a change or attempted change in spatial boundaries, like moving into the space of someone else. Asking these questions is essentially a survival mechanism, and it isn't "bad." He just needs to know the rules he's supposed to follow.

ACTIVATION ZONES AND DEFENSIVE ZONES

Our horses have an innate understanding of these zones and their functions, but for most people, it's something that must be learned. Let's start with the "circles" that each individual is surrounded by: there's a large circle, the activation zone, and a small circle, the defensive zone. When another individual enters the activation zone, they'll be noticed—there's a general, imprecise reaction. However, if they enter the defensive zone, the autonomic nervous system fires up, and innate defensive behaviors are activated. You may recognize this in yourself: when someone stands too close to you, you may hold your breath, clench your teeth, stop blinking, tense up, and more. This is exactly the kind of defensive response you can learn to notice in your horse.

Geometric Patterns

Now we can start to observe the geometric patterns that govern these zones. Learn where your horse's personal zones are through close observation. Start by approaching your horse slowly, in a relaxed manner. Pay close attention to how he reacts. How close are you when he gives you an ear, blinks, or turns toward you? This is his activation zone. Now, start to move closer. How you approach your horse here is important: it matters whether you face him directly or approach him from the side, and whether you do it quickly or slowly. If you approach him slowly, from the side, you can assume he will stay relaxed for a while, because he can see you clearly and he has an open escape route. However, if you suddenly approach your horse head-on, he may hold his breath, stop blinking, and raise his head. In this scenario, he can't see you clearly, and his escape route is directly behind him, in his blind spot, so he can't plan it out. A face-to-face position, among animals and humans alike, can quickly lead to a confrontation. So unless you're looking for a fight, remain calm and friendly, stand at your horse's shoulder, and ask appropriate questions. This way, you'll get a friendly response from your horse.

Define the space where you intend to work with your horse. Create a good learning atmosphere and work slowly. And if things don't work right away, ask your questions more slowly and more carefully, and observe closely how your horse's position in space changes. Praise every little step in the right direction, and stop working on it and step away yourself every now and then, too. Also, work out the best angles for approaching your horse, as well as the best ones for retreating from him. If you ask clear, spatially direct questions, the intention of your movement should resemble motion on a radial line (imagine this line like the spoke on a wheel). This line leads directly from you to the horse. If you approach him head-on, as described, your movement can quickly trigger his body's alarm system. If you move toward your horse at a 45-degree angle, you will find yourself positioned at his shoulder, which gives him the opportunity to find an open door: he can see you with one eye and his escape route with the other eye. If you move in at a 90-degree angle, you will need to cover more distance to approach your horse.

This increase in distance at a 90-degree angle can be perceived as yielding space, and can be a quick way to ease the pressure of the situation for traumatized horses. However, it may also encourage your horse to follow you. Your handling of the space, your choices about both your and your horse's positions in relation to each other, is decisive in establishing whether you can talk to your horse in a way that is easy to understand, or not. Carefully and consciously notice distances and spaces, ask for and give space in equal measure, and help the horse perceive you as predictable and uncomplicated.

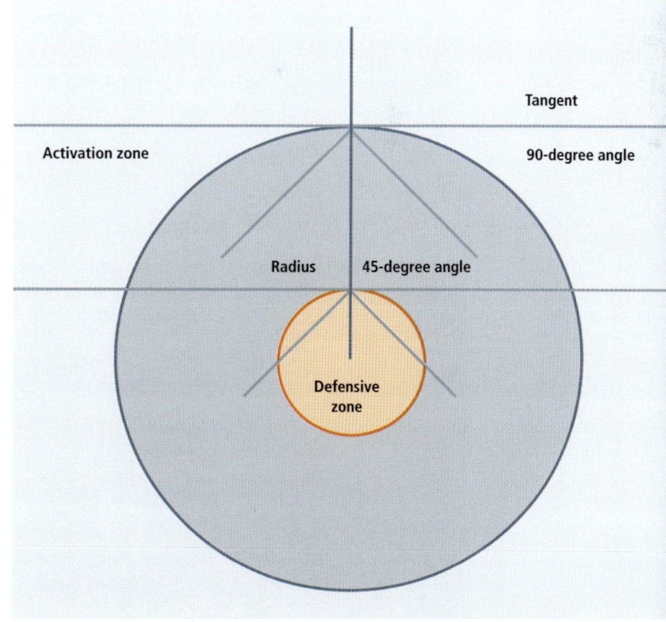

If we always keep the geometric structures involved in our dialogue in mind, we can have a clear, relaxed conversation, and the dialogue will be friendly and subtle.

THE PHYSICAL: BODY LANGUAGE

HORSES READ BETTER

The dream of a harmonious life with our horses sometimes seems unattainable because of conflicts. These conflicts are often the result of misunderstandings, which can arise due to excessive demands or imbalances within a relationship. Believe me, such conflicts happen even in the best situations. This is when it may make sense to get support from a coach.

LEARNING FROM EXPERIENCE

Luca threw her bag in the corner, got on her bike, and headed to the barn to see her horse, Socks. Socks was a five-year-old warmblood, and a real character. Luca was a passionate horse girl. She loved being with horses; they gave her support and security. Or that was how she felt when things went well, at least. When things didn't go her way, despair set in. Socks just asked his questions, which only related to him: more space, more food, more regulation? He never asked how school was, or what was bothering her when she seemed sad. And when she tried to tell him, he didn't listen at all, but just kept asking the same questions all young horses ask. Luca was not yet trained in reading her horse's expressive behavior, but she'd started to realize that something was wrong and their relationship was becoming more difficult.

"Please understand me!" Everyone in a relationship wants to be understood.

Socks could read Luca like an open book. He saw every weakness, every chance to take more space. This made Luca angry, even when she couldn't define exactly what it was that was happening. She would become tense, making defensive gestures without warning, and she often felt too resentful to reward Socks by praising or scratching him. At just 16 years old, she simply couldn't have a holistic view of her dialogue with her horse, or of—for example—the effects of increased tension and the resulting responses. Of course, some people don't even have this ability at the age of 60.

The Teaching Begins

"Hey, stop it." Socks almost pushed Luca over. "Hey, Socks, come on." He yanked her toward a patch of grass, not caring whether she wanted to go with him or not.

We created a classroom, a low-stimulus space, and started together. I instructed Luca: "Try to relax your body; let your shoulders fall and rest one leg when you stand next to him." Socks watched our exercise.

Every coaching session begins with comfort zone training. This relaxes both partners and creates a positive foundation.

"And now start to scratch him." In one hand, Luca held the lead rope quite short, to form a kind of bridge with her forearm to her body. This kept Socks from constantly pushing into her radius so she could work quietly on his rewardability. With her other hand, she scratched his neck. This was done with him positioned along the wall in the arena. As soon as she started, he tried to push her away with his nose. "Defend your space. Stay relaxed, and tell him with a gentle gesture and a 'no' to get out of your space." It's important to note that Luca was able to control her own anger over his behavior. She reacted quickly and with self-awareness. She was a kid with big goals and a real desire to have a relationship with her horse.

Learning to Be Friendly

Luca learned not to react to the threatening behavior of her young horse with aggression. She organized their working space and used her body language in a clear, relaxed way. She understood that if she reacted with anger, she wouldn't be able to become a safe haven for Socks; she would just be an unpredictable adversary who sometimes offered him treats. She wanted to be his friend, so she learned to be friendly. We continued working together. "Start to ask for space now, and gradually move toward his shoulder." Socks lifted his head and tried to stand right in front of her. "Stay right at his shoulder and limit his movement forward with the lead rope. And now take the handle of your riding whip and point it toward his atlas, the first cervical vertebra behind his ears."

Even though she was quite skilled and was able to do everything immediately and correctly, Socks just lifted his head even higher, and looked down at her with a threatening, bulging eye as if to say: "Next time I see you, you're a goner!"

A friendly, unambiguous request for space...

...can be met with resistance.

Relaxed follow-up questions with small steps lead to a resolution.

She needed some encouragement, so I cheered her on: "Keep approaching his shoulder. Don't threaten him; stay friendly, and ask questions." Luca suppressed the lump in her throat, for she sensed that her question hadn't made her horse happy. She didn't yet realize how important this friendly and unambiguous question was to her horse. She would much rather have asked cheerful questions. She would have preferred to yield to him to avoid getting into a fight. "Hang in there," I told her. "Keep asking slowly, and stay at the shoulder." And then Socks took a step backward and gave in. "Stop," I said. "Give him plenty of praise." Luca was relieved when she realized that Socks was beginning to chew. "Good job, you two!"

Each Buckle Is Good Behavior

Luca was a quick learner. Socks, too. There were small rituals between the two of them that sweetened their togetherness. This way, the previously difficult task of tacking up could be completed at a relaxed pace. Every move was rehearsed. Luca introduced reward rituals, and began to praise her horse after each buckle was buckled. In return, Socks started to understand that he should stand still on the cross-ties and not stir up the whole barn aisle with his expectant anger. Every time he was about to paw, Luca quietly said, "No," then walked briefly into his space with increased body tension until he stood still again. Then she consciously took the tension out of her body and went back to her original position. Socks began to trust her; he even began to respect her. Until that time, he had barely tolerated her. Luca began to look forward to spending time with him more and more, because she noticed he was listening to her.

And when she got home from school and hopped on her bike to head to the barn, she already knew what she wanted to talk to Socks about. She also knew that she had the right answers to his questions.

Learning how to communicate in a de-escalating, friendly, and clear way...

...can be helpful in all our relationships, not just when it comes to horses.

SOCKS AND LUCA

Team
Socks, five year-old warmblood gelding
Luca, 16 years old

Expressive behavior:
Closed mouth, no blinking, tension, holding his breath

Purpose/communicative intent:
- pushing
- disrespecting boundaries, lacking emotional and spatial regulation

Training path:
- reading expressive behavior
- using clear communication
- practicing rewardability and responsiveness
- achieving consistency in maintaining boundaries
- maintaining a calm dialogue, expecting calmness while being groomed, being a careful handler

FRIENDLY QUESTIONS

It's an art, not a science, to know how to ask questions in a kind way—especially if they are tough ones—and get an adequate answer. Because of this, it's important that our body language and the pace of our movements are perceived as friendly. To be "friendly" is to use our body language clearly and calmly. We should be non-threatening and completely unaggressive. Luca is not only a lovely person and a dedicated rider, she also has talent. The problem we have here is that an inexperienced person is supposed to train an inexperienced horse. This is a potentially dangerous situation, if the person tries to work on questions they aren't skilled enough to ask correctly. If we humans are not yet able to read the expressive behavior of the horse, then we're already losing: human, zero—horse, one, because remember, he can read our expressive behavior perfectly.

With this in mind, we should be aware of what we are giving the horse to read.

Finding a path together creates relaxation for both partners.

ADJUSTING LANGUAGE FOR THE INDIVIDUAL

Each individual can choose and develop their own physical signals, according to their own abilities. The only thing that must remain consistent is maintaining relaxed body language: you should show no tension, and no threatening or dominant behavior. This way, you can use body tension as a tool for encouragement, and your horse will be able to easily differentiate that signal from your normal, relaxed body language.

BODY LANGUAGE REGULATION

When you're thinking about your body language while working with your horse, imagine that there are different control knobs you can use to adjust:

1. the tempo
2. the tension
3. the intention to move

The first thing to practice is turning each knob down. Consciously move your body more slowly, more softly, and more carefully. Choose a stable position at your horse's shoulder and establish a dialogue with him from there. You can always turn the controls higher at some later point, but this should be a conscious effort, which can be adjusted immediately when the horse's behavior changes.

Although Luca was talented, and learned all her lessons well, she decided she was too young and inexperienced to train a young horse like Socks. She realized she was not yet mature enough to be a good trainer for him, and she knew she needed to learn more herself first. It is incredibly valuable to be able to recognize how much we don't know. Luca understood that real life wasn't like the movie *The Black Stallion*, where an unskilled boy is able to tame a wild horse; she knew the real training had happened off-camera. She made the hard choice to give Socks to someone who could better answer his questions, while she looked for a more suitable horse for herself based on the skills she had. She took full responsibility for herself and did what was best for her horse.

ACOUSTIC LANGUAGE

Keep it short. Keep it simple. Don't get into long-winded arguments with your horse. When we are ranking the various ways to communicate with horses, verbal communication brings up the rear. Our horses don't know or care that we rely heavily on speech and sounds. However, since it's the most valuable link we have between work on the ground and in the saddle, it makes sense to devote time and attention to training with it. What do we want to tell the horse? What signals are going to be important later on when we'll need to direct his attention under saddle.

A DICTIONARY FOR HORSES AND HUMANS

Building a vocabulary to use with your horse can give you important and useful tools. For this "dictionary" you're creating to be helpful, keep the following guidelines in mind:

— You should find it easy to pronounce the words you use.

— Each word used should be as different as possible from the rest; they should sound distinct from one another.

— The words should be at least two syllables if possible, because that way they can be differentiated from each other by their intonation and inflection, not just their phonetic sounds.

— Rhyming words—for example, "go" and "whoa"—can be confusing for a horse. He'll have a hard time hearing the difference between them, especially if they're used in the same command. Clarity is crucial for success.

— Reduce the words you use to what is absolutely necessary; avoid "paraphrasing" or elaborating.

It is difficult for horses to engage with our speech and sounds, and it's a gift that they do it anyway. So stick to the rule of "less is more." Now I'll walk you through the vocabulary I use with my horses, in both physical and spatial language. If you want to truly be able to train in harmony, you'll only be successful if you learn the tricks of the trade and pay attention to the small print.

Nothing is more heartwarming than being on the receiving end of a horse's affection.

☞ A HORSE'S VOCABULARY LIST

PURPOSE	ACOUSTIC	BODY	SPATIAL	MEANING
Learn name	horse's name	relaxed	softly angled	give space turn toward me, give me your attention
Praise	"good," "yes"	soft	hold space	well done, relax
Shift attention	"with me"	slight body tension	hold/request space	I'm about to touch you
	"wait, wait, wait"	slight body tension	hold/request space	you need to change something you're doing, notice your own actions
Initiate walk	"walk on"	angled in the desired direction of movement	walking, requesting and giving space, because it means the horse should start movingl	we're moving, let's go
Stop	"and halt"	stop alongside horse, still angled in direction of movement	stay at the horse's shoulder	we're stopping, whoa
Pick up hoof	"and foot"	stand at horse's side and tap cannon bone	hold space at the horse's shoulder	lift your foot
	"the other one"	tap the other leg	hold your space	lift your other foot
Yield hindquarters	"over"	turn toward the horse	request space	move over (useful when tacking or grooming)
Change of direction longeing or at liberty	"and turn"	turn in the new direction, "close the front door" with the whip if needed	hold or request space as needed	change direction
Trot, longeing or in hand	"and trot"	relaxed	intention directed at the croup	strike off in trot
Canter	"and canter"	relaxed	intention directed at the croup	strike off in canter
Back up	"and back"	held straight, facing the horse	request space	we're backing up
Loading	"load up"	Look inside trailer while standing next to horse	hold space	let's go in the trailer

Say what you mean and mean what you say.

Keep in mind that everything you want to be able to teach the horse later, whether it's a simple task or a difficult "trick," can only be correctly developed if every signal you've already trained the horse to respond to is confirmed and well-understood. Be sure your horse can easily differentiate between the auditory cues you want to give him—each one you teach should have its own distinct sound.

SPEAKING IN RIDDLES

Since we have so many words and synonyms at our disposal, we are very inclined to use them. However, if you use different words for the same thing, or a tone of voice which is arbitrarily harsh sometimes and soft at others, then you create confusion for your horse. In the end, he'll stop listening to your words, and will only read your body language. In this case, when he does what you want, it will probably feel like quite the ego boost, because he will seem to be incredibly in tune with you. However, how often do you think you'll be able to get the right answer from him? If your vocal signals are unclear, how much care are you really taking with how you use body language? Horses are masters at reading bodies, and can react to the slightest changes before we are even aware of them, but we may be unnecessarily confusing.

Consider this situation: You say, "And trot," then you follow up with, "Come on, trot," followed by a click of the tongue, then a smacking sound with the lips, and in the end, "Come on, now, trot." But when the horse is supposed to come to you, the command you've taught is: "Come now." Whatever body language may accompany all these sounds, there's no way the horse can understand what you want. Reduce your language to clear signals and learn to listen to yourself.

☞ YOUR TRAINING DIARY

Write down the signals that are important to you in your training diary and memorize them like vocabulary. A clear, organized vocabulary creates certainty and consistency, which in turn creates trust.

A CLEAR SYSTEM

Make your language a system; learn to express yourself in a way that is easily understood by your horse, with a high degree of consistency and clarity. This can be harder than it sounds. Here is the proof: Have you ever listened as someone raves enthusiastically about something, but shakes their head at the same time? Pay attention to it, and then separate the audio from the image. You'll notice two completely different statements simultaneously.

A successful dialogue is based on both horse and trainer having a willing and open inner attitude.

Animals never do this. Making sure your body language and your words are clear and understandable to your horse is the best way to be a responsible and respectful trainer.

CLEAR, SIMPLE LANGUAGE

When I talk about three-dimensional language, I mean conveying a single message using three different ways of communicating. When I begin a horse's training, I use all three means of communication. As training progresses, I leave one out and check to see whether my question is still understood. If it is, I can leave two out and rely on the single remaining line of communication.

My goal with a riding horse is for the horse to truly understand acoustic signals, because those are the only ones I can take with me into the saddle. If I'm training a horse for liberty work, body language is crucial, and so I reduce communication primarily to visual signals. Clear acoustic control is of course useful here also, but in the cacophony of music and applause that might accompany a liberty demonstration, I won't be able to rely on acoustic signals alone. Spatial language, body language, is especially helpful to a young horse in early training, because they intuitively communicate this way in the herd, so it's the most natural way to begin to create a bond with a horse.

But in all cases, I start with three-dimensional language, and the secret to holistic training is mastering all three ways of expressing yourself. Study them and learn to use all three both simultaneously and separately. It's this clear, consistent use of signals that helps us teach horses in ways they're able to understand.

I like to ride my bicycle with my horses. And honestly, there are very few things more beautiful than watching these magnificent animals running next to me. Proud, strong, and balanced, free and happy, the horses trot at my side—and the relaxation they feel in these moments is an additional benefit in the training. Bicycle training is the culmination of successful communication and generates shared joy in the work. As when riding, I primarily rely on acoustic language here, because cycling limits my ability to use spatial and body language.

To be able to experience this with a horse in all gaits, relying solely on verbal cues, makes me and the horses so happy. I explain how I set up this very special type of liberty work in detail starting on page 164. It demonstrates clearly how a well-developed system of acoustic signals can unify all three forms of communication or separate them, and it shows just how incredibly willing our horses are to work with us. It's up to us to make the best of that willingness.

To understand each other, both must commit to truly listening...

...and this effort to understand each other's signals...

You have a successful dialogue when both partners signal to each other that they're listening.

When in doubt, the horse was right.

DIFFERENTIATING BETWEEN SIGNALS AND AIDS

Let's dive a little deeper into the language we use with our beloved horses. The devil is in the details, but I find it very rewarding to identify potential errors and fix them.

...leads to feeling comfortable in any situation.

LEARNING FROM EXPERIENCE

"This is Fritz," said the young woman, smiling. "I am Nathalie." She was highly motivated and hungry for knowledge. The same could not be said for Fritz. While she told me how kind and sweet he was, the steady-looking Quarter Horse stood next to her, not looking at either one of us. My first impression was of a calm, strong horse. We received no feedback whatsoever with our first attempt at rewardability. All he did was step to the side and swish his tail. "Maybe he doesn't like that?" Nathalie wondered. I assumed he was simply unfamiliar with my approach. This young woman was champing at the bit, so to speak, to work with her horse. My first impression didn't lead me to worry that we would have a real problem with Fritz.

Deciding we could return to rewardability later, I asked her to walk with him. She correctly stood at his shoulder, and had the right tools; she already knew the signals I teach in my book *Wenn Pferde Komplimente machen* [When Horses Bow to You].

It doesn't matter what you look at, it matters what you see.

I was very happy to work with someone so motivated.) She proceeded to say, "Walk on," and simultaneously touched Fritz very lightly on his left hind with the whip. His response: he squeezed his lips together, his nostrils flared, and a bulge appeared above his eyes; he flattened his ears, locked his poll, his tail began swishing, and he raised his croup as if getting ready to kick her. My first impression had been way off, and something was really wrong here.

This wasn't a calm, accepting horse; rather, I suspected passive defensiveness, as shown by his tensing up. The moment they started walking, there was clear identifiable defensive behavior, even signs of aversive aggression in his threatening behavior.

Passive threatening behavior can be missed when we're using driving aids.

Prescription for Defensiveness

Nathalie had sensed that something was wrong, but needed help identifying the main issue. The fact that Fritz refused to accept praise was already defensive behavior that had probably been successful for him in the past. He dodged his handler and swished his tail. He had learned through experience that this was a good way to rid himself of people.

The root of the problem was a simple misunderstanding. This can happen even when people have the best intentions, and is usually caused by nothing more than inexperience. In this scenario, Nathalie immediately used the whip to initiate the walk, because Fritz appeared so steady, and seemed almost lazy. However, by combining the signal "walk on" and the whip immediately, without giving him any warning, Natalie was giving Fritz no chance to avoid the whip by responding first to the verbal signal. Because Nathalie was focused only on driving Fritz forward, she had failed to recognize his threatening responses. He consistently showed defensive behavior (which develops on a purely neurobiological level when someone directly invades a horse's defense zone; see page 61), and because it had been consistently tolerated as a response to her questions, Fritz had essentially been trained to think his defensive behavior counted as a correct answer.

THE LESSON BEGINS

We started by working on awareness. The first step was to read Fritz's expressive behavior without judgment. It was important to me that this young woman be able to hold an independent dialogue with her horse, so I asked her to repeat exactly what she had done before; the only difference would be that instead of continuing to drive him forward, she would simply pay attention to Fritz's reactions.

Nathalie recognized Fritz's signals immediately, and admitted to not really paying attention before: "He's always looked that way. I thought it was just who he was." Maybe the same thing has happened to you. Is it possible you've decided your horse is a certain way, or has a certain personality, and you've stopped being open to really noticing him? Fritz had also formed a firm opinion of people over the years; he had learned that they sometimes used the whip without warning and they could be unpredictable. But Nathalie was sensitive and empathetic—how could she be unpredictable? It was her way of communicating with Fritz that made her seem capricious to him, because she often aimed a stimulus at him without warning. He had no chance to avoid it, which made him dull and sour.

Often, threatening behavior is only taken seriously when it becomes objectionable to the trainer.

Signals and Aids

We approach training from the perspective of questions and answers. Nathalie needed to learn to ask "three-dimensional" questions of her horse, using every means of communication at the same time: the right word, the right movement, and the right body language. And then we practiced the matching aid to support him.

For example, when a horse doesn't immediately react to a signal (which is normal, in the beginning), then that signal needs to be emphasized by a physical aid—in this case, a driving touch or tap—which will carry over into work under saddle. We give him a warning that the tap is coming, so he has a chance to avoid being touched with the whip.

Fritz had never had this chance before, because Nathalie had consistently invaded his defensive zone without warning, which prompted defensive behavior from his sympathetic nervous system; he was stressed by the invasion of his space. This isn't a criticism of Nathalie, or anyone else who may be realizing they have done the same thing—she had no idea she was doing it, and Fritz had no way to know she wasn't doing it deliberately. This is the kind of misunderstanding that happens between humans all the time, too. Perhaps you can see yourself a bit in this situation.

Working with the Traffic Light

We worked on Nathalie's three-dimensional communication using the "traffic light" concept. The goal was, with Fritz, to have him walk off from a verbal cue: "Walk on" (green)—but at first, nothing happened. "Come" (yellow)—still no reaction. Tap with the whip (red)—Fritz used threatening body language, and walked on. "Walk on" (green) then came again, once he was walking on, to help him connect this signal with his actions. Initially, we didn't react to Fritz's defensive behavior, since the first thing we wanted to teach him in this situation was that, from now on, there would be a warning before he got tapped with the whip. I was sure his aggressive behavior would soon disappear.

It only took four attempts before Fritz walked on when he was given a friendly and quiet "walk on" cue, without exhibiting any threatening or defensive behavior. Nathalie showed him she was happy with this answer by generously praising him. Not only had she explained the driving aid to him, she had shown him she was predictable and trustworthy by warning him before escalating with an additional stimulus. By separating the acoustic signal from her extra driving aid (the whip), she made a huge step in the right direction, and all she had to do was change a minor detail. For Fritz, this detail was in no way minor—it was the essential error that needed to be corrected to help them move forward together. This was a small but crucial first step toward exchanging old habits for successful dialogue.

Changing Learned Patterns

Passive defensiveness had become Fritz' established learning pattern over many years; unfortunately, one teaching session wouldn't be enough to fix this learned pattern. Nathalie adjusted how she dealt with him entirely. She became better at identifying situations where she didn't listen to him well enough, where he "shut her up," and where one of them used threatening behavior toward the other. Now that she could recognize it, she was able to respond appropriately to resolve the situation. This is the formula: slower, friendlier, and reward until the praise

Asking the question again in a clearer, friendlier way...

...results in clearer, friendlier responses.

Successful dialogue is the basis for all further lessons, because it creates deep trust.

> *Trust is a gift that animals place in our hands. Handle it with care.*

works. Relying on the principles of the four pillars and giving signals while applying the traffic light concept can make training both clearer and more consistent, which makes for happy people and relaxed horses.

Nathalie began to school Fritz in such a way that the tiniest signal was ultimately successful without any need to follow up with stronger aids. I call this the "Don't Touch" principle (page 104). Once a horse is sensitized to his human, a small signal can be used consistently in any context.

When you are working with a horse, separate your aids from your signals, first on the ground and then in the saddle. If you give a signal for something and there's no reaction to it, then the extra reinforcing aid is given. You probably have a good understanding of the aids for trot, canter, transitions, the half halt, and so on. Try thinking about these aids as signals: canter signal, walk signal, and so on. If you don't get an adequate response to a signal, then a driving aid or a restraining aid is used, following the traffic light principle. It doesn't matter if you want to perform an upward or downward transition. If you want your horse to find his way from canter to trot, give the signal for trot. If the horse doesn't respond to the signal, then ride a half halt and repeat it. Imagine that you want to start trotting rather than that you want to stop cantering. Driving and restraining aids help direct the horse toward the right answer to your signals. I like to call this "riding with signals." Teach your horse

The foundation of liberty work is mutual willingness to engage as well as deep mutual understanding.

FRITZ AND NATHALIE

Team
Fritz, eight-year-old pinto gelding
Nathalie, amateur rider

Expressive behavior:
Phlegmatic, tight mouth, limited blinking, immobile ears; slow, reluctant to move off, swishing tail

Communication issues:
- Defensive responses to praise
- Signs of aversive aggression—behavior intended to pre-empt trainer input
- Refusal to seek a connection with his person

Training path:
- Learn to read the horse's expressive behavior properly and react appropriately
- Develop correct use of questions, driving signals on the ground (following the traffic light principle), and rewardability
- Develop responsiveness and establish boundaries
- Teach leading, communicative longeing, bowing, laying down, liberty work

everything he needs to know by using clear signals. Make sure your signals can be easily differentiated from those extra reinforcing aids that are going to follow an incorrect response to a signal.

Building Happiness

Nathalie understood the natural logic of the language I taught her, and she began to incorporate these conversations every time she handled a horse. She was learning to appreciate the value of slow, thorough communication. Over the course of 18 months, she constructed her own "house" with its four pillars for training in harmony. In just six months, we had established a solid foundation, and we were able to begin schooling "riding with signals." By this point, Fritz had learned to be attuned to Nathalie and to trust her. His whole attitude with her has changed. He bows to her, looks for her, and works with her. Be it at liberty, laying down, or riding, the two of them have become a great team. The defensiveness, misunderstandings, and anger have been completely replaced with a shared joy and a lovely connection in all their work together.

FROM THE GROUND TO THE SADDLE

Two hearts, two minds, and one path. This always leads to the same question, regardless of the age, ability, or goals of the person involved: How do we get a horse to join us on our path, to accept it, to allow himself to be guided by a person, and—in the best case scenario—do it gladly? Some people find it easier to choose and explain a path to the horse from the saddle, and others find it easier from the ground. For the horse, the path of learning these new languages is easiest, gentlest, and most comprehensible when it begins on the ground and later translates to work under saddle. After all, he is used to communicating with other horses on the ground.

STARTING WITH CLEAR DIALOGUE

Let's start a conversation with our horse using groundwork; if this is done correctly, the end result will be a horse who is actively engaged in a dialogue with us. Once he understands our signals, we can take them into the saddle. On the ground, you have the opportunity to really study the horse's expressive behavior, because once you're in the saddle, you can't see things like his nostrils or his eyes. On the other hand, from the saddle we can feel other things much better, such as tension or the horse's intention to move. The combination of good in-hand work and good riding is a recipe for success, because both require unambiguous signals, which, when taught and applied correctly, are the same in both situations. For example, if you want to teach your horse the driving aid, doing so from the ground is much easier, since you are able to read his reactions much more clearly. Then, when you use the same aid under saddle, your horse already knows the right answer to the question you are asking, and you already have a clear idea how he'll react.

CHANNELS OF COMMUNICATION

The order for the signals we use to communicate with our horses is always the same:

1. Acoustic signal
2. Physical signal/body language
3. Spatial signal
4. Acoustic signal

This "sandwiching" of physical and spatial signals between an initial and a final acoustic signal is the sequence used earlier in

Developing strength and straightness results in positive energy for both horse and rider.

my "traffic light" system (page 32). Always think of the fourth signal, the repeated acoustic signal, as a word of praise, and use the appropriate intonation.

No matter which signal I'm teaching the horse, the sequence is always the same.

If you want your horse to trot on the longe, you say, "And trot." If he immediately trots, you praise him by saying, "Good trot." If he doesn't immediately trot off, you say, "Come." He knows this sequence already from being led, and he understands at this point in his training that the next step will be a touch with the whip. If he still doesn't react, you touch his hind end with the lash of the longe whip, use more engaged body language, and move slightly toward his hip in order to encourage him to start trotting. At this point, you repeat softly, "And trot," in a happy, rewarding tone.

Creating a shared language with a horse on the ground...

...is good preparation for work under saddle.

You might be thinking, "I know how to ask my horse to trot," but this sequence leads you to develop quiet, consistent, friendly signals with your horse, with the end result being that your horse listens to you and trusts you. So, even if your horse trots off for you every time, read that paragraph one more time.

THE DEVIL IS IN THE DETAILS

Often, after the first acoustic signal is given, people will immediately use the whip, which they are usually holding in a position where it is constantly present in the horse's field of vision. Additionally, we may find ourselves using a louder and stricter tone of voice—yelling our commands, and often changing the vocabulary as we go. If you want your horse to listen and stay soft, friendly, and motivated, then it makes sense to closely examine the patterns you find yourself engaging in when communicating with your horse. Ask yourself if there's lightness or shared enjoyment in the work.

LEARNING FROM EXPERIENCE

Sophie was a successful, diligent, focused dressage rider. Samson, her Oldenburg, came to her via a few detours. He was often very tense; he was one of those horses with tons of talent but little visible joy. He was unrideable in tests: changing direction, being resistant, even jumping out of the ring. Because helplessness is not fertile ground for trust, Sophie became angry with him. In order to help both her daughter and Samson, Sophie's mother sought out lessons in communication for the two of them.

Respect and Trust in Combination

Sophie had had little success teaching driving aids in the saddle because of Samson's threatening behavior. She had completely missed that the driving aid was not the

Turning with the outside aids provides external balance and inner security for horse and rider.

only problem—they also lacked trust and relaxation. So we began with work in hand to establish trust and respect on the ground first.

I started with the first building block, and by leading on the ground and asking for walk and halt, we found the problem immediately.

It was similar to what I had first seen with Nathalie and Fritz (see page 71), only more defensive and even tighter. Samson reacted to the driving aid on the ground by taking a deep breath and tensing up. He seemed to be trying to brace himself to endure everything. In the next corner, however, he exploded and leapt in the air. Just as with Fritz, Samson didn't get any warning prior to getting tapped the whip. His threatening behavior manifested in him staying virtually frozen and passive one moment only to explode the next. We made a promise to him that he would never again receive a physical signal without a warning first, and that we would try to avoid using the whip altogether. We kept our promise, and we made it a point to reward him as much as we could.

After about six sessions, Samson accepted our praise and started to lick and chew. Eventually, he came to understand the driving aid, and he learned to respond to it without tension. After three months, Sophie and Sampson were again competing: consistently delivering error-free rides with high scores.

Our work on the ground helped Sophie understand her horse, clarify what she wanted from him, and ask in a clear, fair way without succumbing to helplessness. She was able to carry this into her work with him under saddle. She used a specific movement of her pelvis as a signal to walk on: a light pulling forward with her pelvis muscles. At the same time, she said, "Walk on." If nothing happened, she would close her lower leg and say at the same time, "Come," with a gentle touch of the whip.

The moment Samson started to move, she

Exceptional riding is always the result of a subtle dialogue.

took her leg off and gave the same signal as before with her pelvis, in combination with a happy, rewarding-sounding "Walk on."

Essentially, we paired the riding aids with the acoustic signals we'd established on the ground, and applied the aid at the same time as the signal. Pairing the body language used in the saddle with the acoustic signal previously established during ground work creates clarity, which is comforting for the horse. Before I turned my attention to helping Sophie with the aids under saddle, we practiced these steps on the ground until she was very comfortable with the sequence. In this way, Sampson learned to be in front of the driving aids. He learned that he would be praised when he reacted to the signal, but even more so when he reacted to the aid.

Samson began to trust Sophie. His expressive behavior in response to the driving aids changed just as it had during his groundwork lessons. His entire being became more relaxed. He stopped holding his breath; he started blinking. He was a diligent horse, but he had been misunderstood since he had been blocked by the constant activation of his defensive reflexes. We resolved the issue by allowing him to understand what he was being asked. Now he can accept the aids and is reliable in the arena, and he and Sophie are successful at competitions. Sophie won much more with this work than ribbons: she walked away with valuable insights, real knowledge, and a friend.

SAMSON AND SOPHIE

Team

Samson, nine-year-old Oldenburg gelding
Sophie, dressage rider

Expressive behavior:

Closed mouth, unblinking; tension, rigid muscles; holds his breath

Communication issues:

- Activated defensiveness, passive threatening behavior
- Doesn't accept aids
- Shows lack of respect and trust
- Unpredictable reactions to and acceptance of stimuli

Training path:

- Learn to read the horse's expressive behavior and respond appropriately
- Develop acceptance of the aids through ground work
- Work on the lead with use of "traffic light" system
- Establish a dialogue and encourage rewardable behavior
- Explain and confirm driving aids

MISUNDERSTANDINGS CAUSE DEFENSIVENESS

Many horses show defensiveness because they don't understand what's being asked of them. Unfortunately, many people respond to defensive behavior with anger, strictness, and roughness. This leads to increased defensiveness, and in extreme cases can cause the horse to completely shut down. By breaking down the language you use with your horse into its individual components, then combining them judiciously, you can create real understanding

It's worth developing the habit of checking in with your horse for feedback after riding. If he's engaged and responsive to praise, then you know the session went well.

and—ultimately—a true partnership.

CONDITIONED REACTIONS TO STIMULUS

We've all seen it: the rustling of a plastic bag or the sound of a carrot snapping in half, and the horse's ears prick up. The horse's reaction to a sound, long before any treat is given to him, is a conditioned stimulus. The learning process is the same whether the situation following the stimulus is a positive or negative one. For example, the arrival of the veterinarian's car can be a conditioned stimulus signaling the vet's arrival. The horse then walks into the corner of his stall, shows defensive behavior, or tries to escape.

Remember the beautiful Violetta? Her expectant defensiveness was created by a pinching noseband, and bridles became the conditioned stimulus for her defensive behavior. This is just one example that shows that horses listen and observe far better than we sometimes give them credit for; they are always trying to understand the situation they are in, and they pick up every possible signal with their keen senses, whether we are giving it intentionally or not.

ONE QUESTION, ONE ANSWER

A horse's thought processes are linear. The simplicity of this can be an advantage in training if we can resist the very human impulse to create overly complex tasks for our horses. Clear, linear communication helps our horses understand and take responsibility for what we teach. The information we want our animals to understand and respond to should be clear.

Teach the horse that a question always requires an appropriate answer from the ground first. Take this system with you into the saddle, and take responsibility for your own system of communication and how you apply it. Ask for your horse's feedback at the end of training. Work on rewardable behavior and notice his reactions. This is where you can assess how well a training session went from your horse's perspective.

BONDING

— *Be Your Horse's Safe Place*

BASIC TRUST: THE FOUNDATION FOR SECURITY AND CONFIDENCE

The capacity for basic trust is something every living creature carries within themselves, starting at birth. It provides them with the necessary courage to seek food, warmth, and protection the moment after birth, even though they are completely disoriented and helpless. This strong will to live requires a basic level of trust, which can be built upon or chipped away at. Youngsters are also instilled with a natural wariness, which is just as important as trust. This protects young, vulnerable creatures from danger. From the beginning, there's a push and pull between trust and mistrust. The frequency with which one or the other of these instincts gets triggered and reinforced can determine to some degree how trusting or wary an animal becomes, although genetics also play a large role.

A horse's innate ability to bond needs to be carefully encouraged and forever maintained. Nature has a precise blueprint for this.

Bonding doesn't win ribbons, but it's the foundation of trust, and therefore the start to every lesson.

A BREEDING GROUND FOR TRUST

Nature's roadmap requires a calm and protected environment in order for bonding to occur between a dam and her foal. In this setting, basic trust is established, and allows a young animal to bond with his mother and eventually develop self-confidence. In nature, this means they need some distance from the herd: a quiet place to make this very intimate moment of bonding possible.

The moment of birth and the time immediately thereafter is influenced heavily by hormonal changes. Mother and child are able to bond for a few hours and sometimes even a few days after birth. During this window of time, the pair forms what I like to call a "lock and key" bond. This is an unshakable, irreplaceable bond that develops between mother and child, like a lock with only one key. For some animals, this window of opportunity is very small; for others, it is larger.

First, the window closes for the dam, which means that after some time she is no longer willing to accept any other child than her own, meaning the newborn on whom she's imprinted. The newborn remains open to attachment over a significantly longer period of time. This gives the foal a chance at survival even if he should lose his mother: he has a chance to meet another potential mother who is willing to adopt him or will allow him to nurse, and can bond with her.

With our breeding mare Daily Pleasure, we've witnessed the beauty of this kind of bonding. She constantly stays in touch with her son Jupp, either through direct physical contact or acoustically.

Working on bonding emotionally is an incredibly rewarding part of training.

She sniffs him constantly in order to smell him, and she's always attuned to him and ready to shield him from potential danger. Only after several weeks did she allow the "leash" to lengthen, in tiny steps, toward more independence for her little colt. The stronger he got, the more she let him play on his own, but she always kept an eye on him.

Caring for one's offspring is the most primal and unshakable instinct, as it ensures survival of the species. If we as trainers can create a similar sense of attachment with the animals we work with, it can be an invaluable tool in creating a successful partnership.

BEING A SAFE PLACE

Have you ever been able to watch animals bonding? Have you noticed the amount of time a broodmare spends caring for her foal—the intensity and intimacy of the contact; the perpetual sniffing, the tender and constant licking, repositioning, and protecting; the shielding against external danger? Have you ever observed over weeks, months, or even years?

When you bond with your own horse, do you consider the way you handle him? Is it gentle and protective? Or do you just give him a carrot, saddle him, and ride off? Do you hope for a relationship with your horse based on a close bond with him? I'm not trying to be accusatory; I want you to think seriously about this, because if you truly want to build a happy bond, you should want happiness for your horse as much as for yourself.

From a purely physiological perspective, the only way to calm the horse's nervous system when his reflex responses are triggered by a threat is by having a well-established bond with him. My system of training in harmony is based on this simple biological truth. Simply put: If I am a safe place for my animals, then they remain stress-free and happy.

A SPECIAL BOND

I have studied bonds in other animals as well: wild geese, cows, goats, sheep, chickens, cats, and dogs. No matter the animal, the principle behind bonding is the same—it's not just any animal that provides security and protection. It's not just one sheep in a herd, but a particular sheep that another sheep is bonded to that offers comfort. A flock of geese thrives as a group because of the many individual bonds within the flock's structure. Horses also forge individual bonds within the larger herd. I've visited many stables, and have often seen horses grouped together with horses with whom they had no connection, no bond whatsoever. This would never happen in nature. Despite the owner's well-intentioned efforts to mimic a "natural" herd for their horses, they instead created a stressful situation; the limited space and lack of a bond made it difficult for these horses to avoid or resolve conflict through spatial or physical communication.

A real herd is well-structured, not a random group of animals stuck in a shared space.

Rewardability can be reinforced in a variety of situations.

FAMILY BONDS

Our farm has a large herd of sheep as well. When we need to separate out individual animals for medical treatment, the sheep are sorted in a pen that holds about 250 sheep. From there, they go into a "pre-pen," which is much smaller, holding about 15 animals. A small trap door leads to the corridor that goes into this smaller pen. Six to eight sheep fit in the corridor, but only single file. Whenever I look at their ear tags, I see time and again that it's siblings, mothers, and daughters that have walked into the corridor together. They don't lose each other, not even in a tumultuous moment like this, where their herd is being split up and mixed back together. They're joined by a family bond that's multi-generational. I don't think we'll ever learn everything there is to know about this kind of attachment, but I can't stress enough how important it is. It's the basis for building happiness and creating trust. The mother-child relationship not only reinforces the attachment process for offspring, it also lays the groundwork for an animal to form other bonds. It's our responsibility to build on this ability and nurture it further.

GIVE AND TAKE

The need for attachment arises from the functional circle of giving and taking space, of sometimes seeking contact and sometimes driving away, just as we have seen at birth and in the time afterward. This "give and take" needs to be structured and reinforced through good feedback and by establishing limits. Without clear limits and guidance, unregulated attachment behavior can become uncontrollable and uninhibited. It's a push and pull between trust and respect, which allows relationships to become happy, successful, and long-lasting. Nurturing this trust and respect is crucial to creating a strong foundation for future work, where deep trust will be necessary for success. If we as trainers play our part well, we can create a lasting and fruitful bond.

Praise until the praise works—an invaluable exercise in building trust.

BUILDING A BOND

To develop a bond with your horse, you need to provide him with a few key things:

— Social grooming
— Rituals
— Time
— A satisfying physical workload
— A satisfying mental workload
— Spatial regulation
— Loving attention: a horse can never get enough of this

HOW TO RECOGNIZE A HORSE'S EFFORTS TO BOND

You should give good, direct feedback to your horse if he seeks contact with you, smells you, or asks you for scratches. Pay attention to how often your horse is looking at you or turns his body toward you, and when he is focused on you. Spend time with him in his stall, as well as in his paddock or pasture. Make your interactions with him positive; reward his attention with active praise, and don't ignore his attempts at contact.

WHAT CAN DISCOURAGE A BOND?

A horse's willingness to try to form a bond with you can easily be discouraged by defensive, harsh treatment, but can also be affected by frequent upheaval in his living conditions, such as moving to a new farm, a change in handlers (including staff), a change in his herd, or even a change of social partners. Most commonly, however, attachment is subtly chipped away, simply through our failure to respond to a horse's attempts to bond. If you don't acknowledge your horse's efforts to connect, these moments will become quieter and quieter, rarer and rarer, and at some point they disappear completely. There are horses that are easier to bond with, and there are those who are more reluctant to initiate. With these more reserved horses, don't just accept this as the status quo! Work hard to build a bond.

HOW CAN A DAMAGED BOND BE REPAIRED?

Devote the necessary time to the activities that I am about to describe here. They may seem like small, trivial things, but they'll help you develop a true bond. Treats can seem like an easy way to "buy" a horse's affection. Of course, a carrot or apple as a treat can be a great help with a horse that has a hard mouth—it's useful to get them chewing. But remember that an honest bond, when correctly established, has no drawbacks. Treats can make your horse beg, and you may eventually find yourself negotiating a slippery slope of food as reward, or "pay for work." This can't be considered progress in training or bonding, because a demanding horse tends to show a lack of respect for proper boundaries. Consider employing the following methods instead.

PRAISE UNTIL THE PRAISE WORKS

Consider every possible aspect of bonding, and have frequent, consistent contact with your horse. Remember the guiding principle of my system: Praise until the praise works.

This alone is the first step toward an honest relationship. Create time and space in which you only work on praise and rewardability—don't be in a rush, and don't set any expectations. Just give yourself and your horse some quality time. If someone wonders why you're spending so much time with your hands deep in his coat, just tell them you're working on your relationship with him. Be proud of this kind of training, because it's a direct path to real friendship.

Start exercising both your body and your horse's. All horses need regular exercise. This, too, can build bonds. Healthy riding, communicative longeing (page 167), and liberty work all help with bonding. Make a commitment to your horse: stick to a regular schedule, and offer your horse clear, unambiguous communication he can rely on. This creates trust, and is exactly what's needed for bonding.

Attachment training is like caring for a plant: it needs time to grow and regular care. So please don't expect to cross this step off your training schedule any time soon. You'll only become a safe place for your horse by spending the necessary time on allowing him to decide that that is what you are.

Every horse has a favorite scratching spot, which can be anywhere on his body.

Scratching is part of natural grooming behavior and leads to the release of relaxing hormones.

HORSES AND LONELINESS

"The heart has its reasons which reason does not know."

—Blaise Pascal

Consider the life of an average sport horse: for the first six months, the foal is allowed to be with his mother, before he's weaned and sent off to join a herd of similarly-aged youngsters who are all strangers to him. This is the first massive break in the bonding system: a new place and strange new herdmates. Around two and a half or three, the horse is sent to a trainer, where he's probably kept alone. He's now lost his former herd. By age four or five, he's sold as a competition horse, and needs to cope with his owner's active show schedule.

He has no social bonds; the people around him change because no one works every day of the week, so he meets new people all the time. In a situation like this, bonding can't be nurtured, and equilibrium between his instincts for trust and wariness can't be established, either. How is a horse in this situation supposed to be able to bond?

A touching moment—mother and daughter meet again after two and a half years.

BONDING, A PRINCIPLE OF LIVING

The dark bay mare Violetta, whom you met earlier in this book, came to us a few years ago. A year later, her daughter also arrived at our farm. The two had been separated for two and a half years—but it only took a few seconds of contact for them to bond again. This moment was striking and almost magical, and proved once again that the bond between mother and child is enduring and incredibly strong. It was a true joy to be able to allow them to live together again.

Horses who find someone who offers love, understanding, and competence are incredibly lucky.

LEARNING FROM EXPERIENCE

Picco had won the lottery; he just didn't know it yet. He was in a new stable with new people, who were absolutely crazy for horses. From now on, this ten-year-old Westfalen gelding would be cared for with consistency and love.

Picco's life up until this point had been a typical one, with all the accompanying difficulties. Although his new life was a virtual paradise, he was withdrawn and passive. He wasn't curious, and he didn't seek contact with anyone. He seemed uncomplicated, and made no demands. When ridden, he was insecure: he didn't like to go on the trails by himself and wanted to return to the barn quickly. He was tense, and always held his mouth shut and his head high.

His new owner Regina suspected he was lonely, and although he listened well, he didn't *communicate*. She started to try different things when she worked with him, searching for a way to open a dialogue with him. With this in mind, she focused on bonding with him, and tried to encourage him to give reasonable responses.

It took over a year before Picco relaxed when he was praised, before he would drop his head and relax his neck, and before he started to lick and chew. Essentially, it took over a year before he trusted Regina—but she was very patient. She understood the importance of bonding, and refused to abandon him to his loneliness.

Direction, Space, Regulation

Because Regina had no desire to compete, she spent most of her time working on bonding with Picco. This doesn't mean she spent all her time cuddling. She worked on leading Picco in a consistent manner, turning him, and requesting and giving space. She worked on rewardability in a safe environment, searching his body for his favorite scratching spots. She trained him in communication (page 167) and in classical longeing. She worked with him on the ground, including at liberty. He was soon able to bow, lie down, and lie flat. Regina's background was in classical dressage, but she had already learned that the conventional way of doing things could benefit from establishing a successful dialogue. Having trained two horses before learning and using my system, she already understood the importance of working in harmony with her horse.

Three Years on the Path to Happiness

Three years have passed since Picco and Regina came to me. He now looks for Regina and happily participates in his training. He blinks, has a soft mouth, and drops his head; he's the picture of relaxation. He comes when she calls him, lies down when she asks, and plays every game he's asked to play. He trusts her when they go out on the trails, which means he's happy to hack out in the countryside.

He does all this for his human because he has a bond with her now. He gave Regina his trust, which she accepted as the gift that it is, never blaming him for his mistakes. Every inch along their path together is worthwhile progress. Until Regina entered his life, Picco was adrift and alone.

Earning a horse's trust sometimes requires patience, but it's always time well spent.

PICCO AND REGINA

Team:
Picco, ten-year-old Westfalen gelding
Regina, accomplished dressage rider

Expressive behavior:
Seeking little to no contact; no blinking, closed mouth, high head; withdrawn, insecure

Communication issues:
— Passive

Training path:
— Learn to read expressive behavior and react appropriately
— Start bonding training
— Search for ways to create dialogue
— Nurture rewardability
— Manage space

Proximity and distance are important elements of spatial language.

TIME CAN'T MATTER

Picco is a perfect example of the kinds of signals we shouldn't ignore. If we sense that something isn't going well—that the horse is tense, withdrawn, or difficult to praise—then these are the lessons that have to come first, that must have priority. When rebuilding a horse's willingness to bond, time cannot matter. I often hear my students say they tried to work on rewardability, but their horses didn't like it. I always answer the same way: "If it hasn't worked yet, you're not done. Keep praising him, more earnestly, and find a quieter setting to work in."

How long it takes to rebuild the horse's willingness to bond or build a new bond varies from team to team. If you work on praising a horse and notice he relaxes quickly, you are on the right track. If, however, you have a horse that turns away, acts threatening, or gets tense, then your work has just begun. Work with his spatial language, give him direction, and set boundaries. If you work on these things while reinforcing his rewardability through systematic praise, he'll start to become more willing and more able to bond with you. Many horses are so thoroughly conditioned to work only for "pay" (food) that they hide their loneliness behind an appearance of responsiveness. However, treats cannot take the place of a genuine bond. Food rewards can help establish a bond if they're used correctly and in moderation (for example, to motivate the horse to soften his mouth and chew).

Horses whose instinct toward wariness has overpowered their instinct toward trust because they spend their lives in solitude can easily overreact. They may have a short fuse or become unpredictable. Nurturing and developing their willingness to bond, therefore, should always be your first priority.

THE ROAD TO SUCCESS

We celebrated my daughter Carla's first victory in advanced dressage, on our Oldenburg stallion Fuerstenkind, with laughter and champagne. Carla had already achieved a lot in dressage, and although each win was special, the first victory in the advanced class was truly meaningful. And so we toasted to twelve years of daily teamwork: training, cold feet, getting up in the middle of the night for braiding, learning the lessons for hours, and shivering in the cold standing next to the warm-up arena. Twelve years, going from training level to FEI with a horse we had bought as a shaggy weanling—he had been half blind in one eye due to an accident, and we raised and trained him ourselves.

Back then, when we bought this gangly, visually impaired little horse, we said we could give him security. Today he gives us security. With his huge heart, Fuerstenkind has learned everything we've taught him: leading, yielding, bowing, lying down, lying flat, sitting, loading; competing alongside goats and ducks, with spotlights and music; working at liberty; water training, travers, flying changes, pirouettes, and piaffe. This special stallion was so willing to try what we asked of him.

A HOLISTIC MANAGEMENT PROGRAM

And as we sipped our champagne and enjoyed the moment, those twelve years seemed to have flown by; we could only hope for more time ahead for this rider and horse we had trained. We were successful because we had a passionate rider and a good horse, as well as clear goals and a good system. I can still hear myself repeating: "Hang in there, we can do it." "Don't worry about mistakes, we'll do better next time." "Control your ambition, and feel your horse." "Learn from failure; disappointment comes with the territory." "You did that really well." I filmed every test to review afterwards, although for some tests I was so nervous that all I filmed was the footing.

The happiest people do not have the best of everything, they make the best of everything.

Success in competition comes from excellent basics, but partnership and genuine friendship should be the real motivation for correct training.

Since then, I've become more resilient, as has Fuerstenkind. I still have fond memories of our very first ride in the Meller mountains. It's a steep climb. "Fuersti" was three years old then, and halfway up, I got off to make it easier for him. Today he sees the mountain, goes into four-wheel drive, and in no time we're on top of that hill.

Fuerstenkind learned to listen early on. Since he has a healthy tendency toward steadiness, and tends to be a little lazy, we made his training engaging and versatile. This meant he was sometimes ridiculed by others in the sports scene around us. "Oh, he also does circus tricks, I see..." Yes, if real connection, groundwork, gymnastics, trust work, bonding work, and liberty work are "circus tricks," then he is certainly doing "circus tricks."

WINNING AS A TEAM

In addition to these tricks, he accompanied Carla from training level to FEI dressage. It was exclusively Carla, a teenager, who showed with this stallion, which is a testament to the hard work of our entire team. It takes so much work to get a horse to the point where he is so strong, so beautiful, and so willing to work. There are so many pieces to the puzzle, and sometimes after taking one step forward, we took two back. I'm so grateful to be able to do this kind of work. The development of his body, his mind, and his relationship with us enabled our Fuerstenkind to choose to respond to us—because he knows he is not alone, he knows someone is listening to him, and he knows he's physically and mentally strong enough for the task at hand.

The guiding principle of training in harmony: Praise until the praise works.

FIT FOR THE SPORT

A fitness program for the horse involves more than longeing and riding in the ring: it should take into account whole-body mobility, nutrition, and overall management, and shouldn't be overly complicated or unfocused. Whether it's climbing hills, moving through water, working over cavaletti, or hacking out, everything that builds muscles should be in our horse's workout program.

At least, that's how we do it at our farm. We're lucky to be able to train our horses with a little bit of everything. There's a pond where we can swim with our horses, or supervise them from the edge while they swim. We also have access to a second pond with water only one or two feet deep, with an island we can stand on if we want to longe. To build strength, we can go to the mountains as often as possible for long rides uphill, alternating between trot and canter. We also practice gymnastics in hand, and ride movements (from transitions to pirouettes) with an eye toward building strength.

For us, strength training is mental and physical. It's about versatility, motivation, and health. Quite simply, a horse needs strength to carry us and withstand stressors. A mentally strong horse has a good bond with his trainer, which helps him process requests. As your horse's personal trainer, your work with him should be both comprehensive and versatile; it should incorporate the training elements that best suit you as a pair.

Athletic achievement and fun can go hand-in-hand.

INTERVAL TRAINING

For our Fuersti, interval training has always been the most successful approach. We alternate short performance phases with long walk breaks. These breaks allow his muscles to rest while still keeping him mentally engaged. While working at the walk, we can check his overall responsiveness: his responsiveness to the outside aids, obedience to the leg, and softness in the poll. This is achieved through frequent re-positioning and bending, by switching between lateral movements and straightness, by halting and reining back, and by taking time for praise. We can ask for haunches-in and swing it into shoulder-in, or for quarter, half, or full pirouettes, or simply alternate flexion or bend between true and counter-positioning.

I love to take advantage of long walking intervals to play question-answer games.

Working toward shared goals with playful consistency.

Cross training can broaden the horizon for both horse and rider.

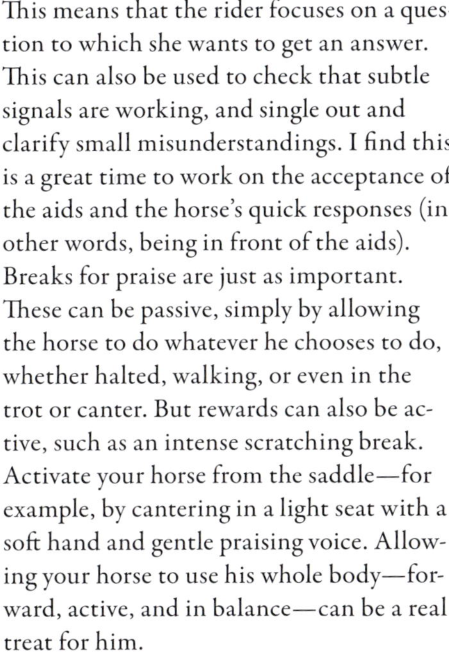

This means that the rider focuses on a question to which she wants to get an answer. This can also be used to check that subtle signals are working, and single out and clarify small misunderstandings. I find this is a great time to work on the acceptance of the aids and the horse's quick responses (in other words, being in front of the aids). Breaks for praise are just as important. These can be passive, simply by allowing the horse to do whatever he chooses to do, whether halted, walking, or even in the trot or canter. But rewards can also be active, such as an intense scratching break. Activate your horse from the saddle—for example, by cantering in a light seat with a soft hand and gentle praising voice. Allowing your horse to use his whole body—forward, active, and in balance—can be a real treat for him.

THE PERFORMANCE CURVE

Build intervals into your training, whether on the ground or under saddle. Pay attention to the performance curve within each session. Each session will have a peak; you'll notice the moment. The horse will feel motivated, there will be positive energy, and you and your horse will be "clicking." If you keep working and notice that these "peaks" aren't as obvious anymore, then it's time for a break. I could always ask my daughter whether she wanted to keep going, but not Fuersti; we had to be careful to make sure he didn't ignore his own physical limitations in his constant attempts to please us.

A good time for a break is when you're working on the "uphill" side of the performance curve. In my system, horse and rider are artists. True artistry means the work is never forced, and always stops when it is at its best.

Be fresh for the hard work, and stop when it's at its best.

WARM-UP IN THREE PARTS

The start of training has three components:

1. Emotional: we establish rewardability and therefore, inner relaxation.
2. Cognitive: we play the question-answer game, asking easy questions and expecting immediate responses.
3. Physical: we ride a gradual warm-up.

We ask for canter only after the horse has been allowed to trot in a long and low frame, moving from back to front and swinging over his back. After the warm-up canter, the horse is given a walk break, which includes praise and standing breaks. Only after a productive warm-up and rest-reward period is the horse put into the training phase of the ride. This is where a new task can be introduced, or a big new question about a current training goal can be asked.

For horse and rider, these intervals, the achievable goals and learning steps, are so important, but just as important are the standing breaks: stop and praise until the praise works.

A wonderful, successful team.

The strength that Fuersti built up over the years never seemed to be quite enough. It didn't help that he was a bit lazy. We had to find creative ways to develop him. It wasn't enough to just stack up training rides. Muscle strength, strong nerves, endurance, and diligence are all part of what makes a good dressage horse and athletic partner.

Just as you expect your horse to be fit for his job, we as riders need to keep an eye on our own nutrition and athleticism. When both horse and rider are able to work as a team, the feeling of strength and power is indescribable. When Fuersti's strong body lifts up during the canter depart or in the pirouettes, or when we ride half-halts, it feels almost as if he is about to take off into flight. It makes you feel like you are in a Ferrari.

MULTIFACETED STRENGTH TRAINING

In order to maintain your horse's health, the need for strength training is clear. If we're not careful, Fuersti can become very plump. Since the way to a horse's heart can pass right through the stomach, it can be a challenge for anyone to keep a beloved horse in top shape. This is why it's so important to create a goal-oriented and multi-faceted training plan.

Make your program as varied as possible; do something different every day. Asking a horse to lie down or bow is like asking him for push-ups, and training in water is a holistic approach to fitness: it strengthens the horse's back and his ability to carry. While swimming provides all-around muscle building, cavaletti work promotes balance and dexterity. We should make every effort to make the horse's daily activity as well-rounded as possible. If he were able to live in the wild, he would have all the muscle and dexterity he'd need, as well as constant communication and bonding experiences.

None of us knew it was possible to love a horse this much.

☞YOUR TRAINING DIARY

In a journal, keep a record of your personal training program and how to best keep your horse fit. This way, you'll be able to:

— Keep a record of your training.
— Check that you're varying the workouts.
— Optimize your time spent training.
— Watch the performance curve by having a record of your horse's progress. This allows you to track your horse's cognitive and physical abilities and offer breaks while still on the uphill side of the curve.
— Check your own physical fitness.
— Remember that training is a combination of building both fitness and communication skills.

Keeping a daily diary is an excellent way to track what you are doing and notice overarching patterns, which allows you to optimize your individual training plan.

THE POWER OF LOVE AND ATTENTION

Every day here is defined by our work with and around horses, and although each has held a place in my heart, I had no idea that it was possible to love a horse as much as we love Fuerstenkind. Carla has helped to develop many horses and has been a witness to their history and development, but none has been as special to her as he has been. As much joy as I feel riding him, the best thing by far is to see Carla and Fuersti together. The harmony between this lovely rider and powerful horse is, to me, perfection. I know I'm biased, but I'm not just a coach and partner here, I'm also a mother. Having a horse as a true friend is a special gift. Although Carla sat on a horse before she could even walk, her relationship with our stallion is something entirely different and remarkable.

Believe in your horse; believe in yourself.

Once you have a horse on your side, he'll do anything for you.

He doesn't give her anything for free, but when she asks correctly, he gives her everything.

Carla isn't naive. She understood that others with more expensive horses that were fully trained had surpassed her. But she also knows through our work together that it's worthwhile to put your faith in your horse, in yourself, and in our system. Maybe Fuersti is not the cream of the crop of dressage horses, but a whole family lives in his heart, and Carla can know the joy of having a singular bond with him.

BONDING SYSTEM VS. DEFENSIVE SYSTEM

Not every horse is lucky enough to have a clear path laid out for them. In Fuerstenkind's case, his bonding system had always been supported and nurtured. He's a lucky guy who grew up in our system of training in harmony. But what if fate is unkind, and a horse not only has to endure being confused and misunderstood, but finds that his only escape is to give up and withdraw into himself? What if he becomes unpredictable and refuses to engage anymore? Maybe you've met a horse that always stands with his head in the corner, where every encounter is filled with negative anticipation and massive defensiveness, and the goals you set can't be reached. Horses that no longer see—this is how I describe these horses whose eyes look empty, who no longer seek contact and turn away from people and from life. If a horse meets every request with defensive behavior—then what?

LEARNING FROM EXPERIENCE

"You have to help us. He jumps well, but he's getting more and more difficult to mount. It's getting dangerous," my friend told me. He was talking about a young jumper that had recently moved into his stable. His trainer, Charlotte, had already fallen several times while trying to mount.

I decided to make a house call to meet this big bay horse named Hermann. When we arrived, he was standing in the corner of his well-maintained stall. I walked in and immediately realized it wasn't going to be easy to approach him. He held his breath, turned his croup toward me, stopped blinking, and clamped his tail and his jaw. His entire being emanated defensiveness. We brought him into the aisle and cross-tied him so I could look carefully at his entire body.

He acted as if he had been struck by

lightning when I touched him. He jerked violently and tried to move away from me.

Charlotte, a cheerful person by nature, believed in Hermann, as did my friend. It was difficult for her to see how the gelding had become more and more isolated. He was new to them both, and they didn't know much about him other than that somebody had done some driving with him and he had been successful at a few jumper shows, which made him an interesting prospect.

Sometimes, you need to hit the reset button with bonding...

...no matter how long it takes.

Bonding—Starting Over

We decided to hit the reset button and start from the beginning with Hermann. Riding was replaced with bonding work instead. The plan was for Charlotte to place a bowl with carrots and apples in front of Hermann's stall; everyone who passed his stall would feed him something. You may be wondering why I consider treats not just okay in this situation, but the first step. You're right, I don't like to rely on food as a reward—but in this case, we had to rebuild trust from the ground up. Hermann needed to learn to associate people with something nice. Charlotte quickly learned my system for leading a horse (page 166) and practiced every day with him. At the same time, she worked to discover his favorite scratching spots.

It took a few weeks before Hermann's defensive system calmed down. We trained systematically, but riding remained out of the question. Charlotte loved jumping, but her main priority was the horse's well-being, not just quick success. She lured him into engaging with her, and gradually won him over. She noticed some changes immediately. He started standing at the front of his stall looking for her—working on bonding was fun for both of them. After a few sessions, we decided to try to re-introduce riding. Charlotte tacked up Hermann and brought him into the arena, but his expressive behavior was obvious right away: he held his breath, pinched his nostrils, and refused to blink. His ears were unmoving, his back tense, his tail clamped, and his head held high.

"Not today," we said, laughing, because it was pretty clear that Hermann wasn't on board with our plan. I'm sure this was the exact moment where the original mistake had been made with him. He stood very still, and this had clearly been enough for the people who'd started him. Nobody had noticed his passively defensive behavior.

Changing One Variable at a Time

We spent some time longeing him with his saddle on (see page 167). This kind of longeing is about dialogue, about questions and answers, and about ignoring external distractions. He participated happily, dropping his head more and more and also demonstrating more and more acceptance of bonding; primarily, we made sure to give him consistent breaks for praise. In order to teach Hermann how to deal with stressors, we changed the training by gradually introducing new elements. Changing one variable at a time, we put a blanket on his back, laid down poles and cavaletti, and even tied large jollyballs to his saddle. We always gave him as much time as he needed, and worked with him until he accepted the new element, which we could recognize by his breathing, his level of relaxation, and his blinking eyes. This helped him learn how to process and cope with new stressors.

HERMANN AND CHARLOTTE

Team:
Hermann, seven-year-old Bavarian Warmblood gelding, jumper
Charlotte, trainer

Expressive behavior:
Whole-body defensiveness: breath held, clamped tail, unblinking eyes, lips tight

Communication issues:
— defensive, passively threatening

Training path:
— Learn to read expressive behavior and react appropriately
— Reduce demands
— Build a bond
— Develop a clear means of communication
— Allow space for the horse to take the necessary time to understand and take direction, and establish clear rules: the next question gets only asked after the horse accepts and answers the current one

Letting Go Starts in the Mind

Hermann was truly lucky to find himself with Charlotte. She was so sincerely pleased with each small bit of progress. She shared her joy not just with me, but also with him. She took her time with him, and was always willing to take a step back rather than push onward. She benefited so much from training in harmony, because she now recognized his expressive behavior much faster and, most importantly, more objectively. She listened to him and took his signals seriously. His defensive behavior disappeared little by little, and he began to make active offers. During work in-hand and at liberty, she was able to manage his tempo and use of space. When it came to rewardability, she was able to give him comfort, and he became more attentive in his responsiveness.

A Safe Environment

In addition, Charlotte made sure Hermann got a permanent social partner, a real buddy who could offer him companionship and comfort. Not only did she work to give him the best overall care and diet, she began to adjust every minor detail that was important to him. After the first few weeks of training, we had Hermann on our side. We practiced mounting just for the sake of mounting, with no intention of riding him. When Charlotte had one foot in the stirrup, we watched his reaction. As soon as he stopped blinking, we stopped where we were, and praised him until his sympathetic nervous system calmed down.

Only then did Charlotte take her foot out of the stirrup. Yes, this is how small the steps were.

But that's the whole point: If you truly want to train in harmony and build a happy bond with your horses, you need to succeed first with the small things, and develop a feel for timing and pacing. Learn to ask questions of your horse with harmony and relaxation as your guiding principle. Learn to embrace the idea of taking a few steps backward to get ahead, and incorporate breaks. Be sure your horse can understand you and only proceed if you have his acceptance. Some horses are quite straightforward; some are not.

With Hermann, we spent an entire hour just mounting, dismounting, and rewarding him. This hour was critical in helping Hermann start trusting us. The next day, Charlotte sent me a photo of her sitting on top of Hermann: she was out hacking, in shorts and bareback. My first reaction was to feel a bit angry with her (because this can be dangerous!), but then I realized Charlotte was a great student; she had learned to listen to her horse, so there was nothing to worry about. I was so happy for them both. From that moment on, a partnership began that sometimes brought tears to my eyes. Once Charlotte was able to begin riding Hermann, their progress was steady. She started training him over fences, and soon they were successfully competing. Hermann began to fight for her. He repaid all she had done for him with compound interest.

Targeted work on the basics gives the horse confidence and creates a safer situation for both horse and rider.

In a Nutshell

Hermann's ability to bond had been completely atrophied, and his defensive system was overactive. He had begun to develop expectant defensive behavior: getting rid of the rider immediately was, to him, the best option. He wasn't trying to injure anyone—he was simply unable to express his unhappiness any other way. The resulting helplessness of the people around him only served to increase his loneliness even more. His ability to bond risked complete shutdown. This can have dire consequences for everyone involved, and training errors at this point are sadly common. Even trainers with the best intentions can end up producing angry, stressed, shut-down horses by not listening to them. Hermann is not just a lucky guy, he's also lovely to behold, because now his personality shines bright.

The whole training path for Hermann and Charlotte took about six months. Although Charlotte never gave up on her goal to compete Hermann, she put it aside to show this horse that she wouldn't give up on him either. She won him over by opening a dialogue with him on the ground, which then allowed her to do the same from the saddle. Anyone who understands that riding is a conversation and horses aren't just a four-legged means of transportation will happily ask their horses questions and listen for the answers.

SIGNALS AND AIDS

In riding, I differentiate between signals and aids. Exceptional riding is defined by quiet signals, and doesn't require any aids. Next time you're riding and you ask your horse for the walk, pay attention to what earns your horse's response. Is it the leg aid, pushing forward with your pelvis, or you using your spurs?

Let's think it through:

1. If you combine the slight forward movement of your pelvis with the verbal cue, "Walk on," then you're using the same signal your horse learned on the ground. Let's imagine your horse doesn't respond.
2. Now, as a warning, quietly add your leg. This corresponds to the signal, "Come," on the ground, which was the yellow phase of your traffic light. Then, if you still get no response, gently touch your horse's croup with the whip until he starts to walk on.
3. At that moment, push your pelvis slightly forward again. This tells him, "That means 'walk on'."

This is only one of many signals your horse will learn. There are signals to ask for trot, canter, halt, rein back, lateral work, turns, collection, and so on. The aids, meaning the driving aids and the restraining aids, serve only to emphasize your signals and direct the horse in case he doesn't immediately find the correct answer to your question. It is consistently the same as on the ground: reliable, careful, and light.

ACCEPTING THE AIDS

One of the most important steps in this process is acceptance of the aids. In training young horses, the experienced trainer must always try to keep this in the foreground, because if a horse doesn't accept or respect an aid, then that aid can't help the horse find the correct answer.

Exceptional riding is based on a horse's relaxed and prompt acceptance of the aids and systematic signals. If you feel the beginnings of resistance or defensive behavior in response to your aid, then make a concerted effort to ensure the aid in question is respected and accepted. Forget whatever else you had planned to work on that day, and prioritize understanding and giving the correct response to your signals and aids.

Remember, the goal is always to abide by the "Don't Touch" principle, meaning your signal should be enough instruction for your horse, and the aid should be unnecessary in the end. This principle means we will eventually be able to reduce the signals we use with the horse to their simplest form. It teaches the rider to give subtle signals, and tests the horse's ability to listen well.

Mutual trust can be particularly important in some cases.

LEARNING FROM EXPERIENCE

I had an Instagram friendship with a young equestrian named Gianna; I followed her, and she followed me back. Gianna is a para rider, and she has a wonderful dark bay mare named Selma. Due to an accident, Gianna lost the use of her legs, and she relies on a wheelchair. She often posted about her riding, and I liked what I saw, but even more than that, I was touched by her positivity and confidence. I decided to invite her to visit our farm, and she happily accepted. When she arrived with her partner and her dog, it immediately became apparent that we had similar goals. I showed her most of the farm, but it was too muddy for her to reach the ponds in her wheelchair. So I asked her if she'd like to ride our stallion Fuerstenkind, and her eyes lit up.

A Different Approach to Mounting

We took Fuersti out of his stall and tacked him up, and then I showed her how to ask a horse to lie down. It was his first time doing this for a stranger. On top of that, he'd never seen a wheelchair up close before. Fuersti looked at me, then at Gianna, measured the distances, and lay down more carefully than he ever had before in his life. Gianna's spatial and body language was definitely different from what he was used to, but her acoustic signal was the same, and he had learned to listen. I had to pretend I got dust in my eyes. It was powerful to see that my horse, a stallion who was only ten years old, trusted me enough to do what was asked of him despite the unusual circumstances.

I never doubted that he would answer the question, but it was touching to see how well he wanted to do it.

His calm attitude as he waited gave Gianna the confidence she needed to climb, on her own, onto an unfamiliar horse. Fuersti waited for both of us to have everything sorted out, and then Gianna asked him to stand. I think I heard a squeal of joy as Fuersti carefully stood up and then stood still, waiting. When we went to the ponds and looked at everything, I'm not sure if Gianna really saw anything, because she only had eyes for my sweet Fuersti.

Confidence and Self-Awareness

Gianna brought her mare Selma to train with me for a while. Since she rides without the use of her legs, she needs clear signals to make herself understood by her horse without the use of strength and spurs. Because of this, my system of training a horse to respond to signals rather than aids fit very well with her ideas about riding and horsemanship. Gianna rode with two whips, using them in lieu of leg aids. (I also occasionally ride with two whips, because it can help the horse improve his balance.)

Gianna hoped Selma would learn to lie down. She was a great mare with a strong character who had gone through thick and thin with Gianna. Since Gianna had already taught Selma very well to listen to her, pay attention, and be mindful, the work went very quickly. When we started by teaching leading and bowing, one question that still needed to be answered was about requesting space.

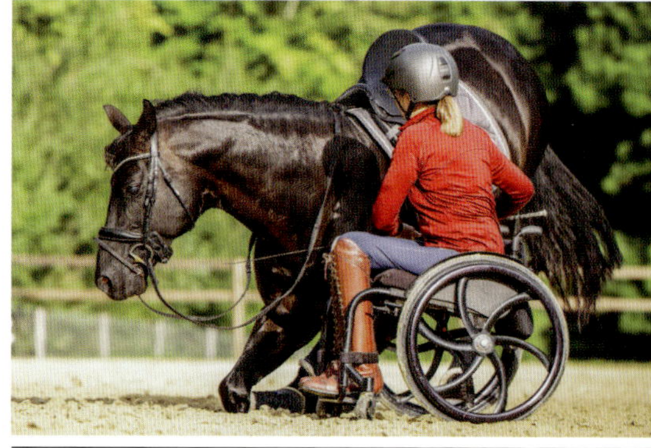

Fuerstenkind is careful and responsible with Gianna....

...which gives her a sense of security and helps her trust him.

Horses can make humans truly happy.

Selma hadn't learned this, because Gianna couldn't give and ask for space as fast as Selma needed. Gianna and Selma were a pair who had more than just made it through their honeymoon phase. They were faithful to each other, but Selma lacked the last bit of confidence she needed to relax when asked to lie down. Both horse and rider needed the confidence and self-awareness to calmly approach this question and its answer correctly.

Time Can't Matter

Selma learned the movement and understood what was being asked of her when she was asked to lie down, but she would immediately shoot back up. Lying down requires a great deal of trust, and if it's going to be beautiful and right, it only works if the horse has a relaxed inner attitude. This was what Selma needed time for; she and Gianna had a wonderful relationship, but here Gianna was in a bit of a hurry, and had to find her own inner peace. It can be tempting to rush when we're uncertain or worried.

What do I do if my horse doesn't want to lie down? I give him the time he needs until he is comfortable with the idea. During this time, lying down is practiced at a steady pace. The horse is always free to get back up, and he should never be coerced or held down. Only when horses understand this can they trust us enough to volunteer to lie down. If they do get back up before I want them to, I quietly ask them to lie down again. In my book *Wenn Pferde Komplimente machen* [When Horses Bow to You], I describe in detail how to do this. But here I want to focus on the dialogue and the framework we set up for the horses. Selma needed a lot of space—temporal space, time to process. We practiced until Gianna was able to do it correctly, and then we decided to wait for Selma, as we had learned from Fuersti how good it feels when someone waits for you.

Fuersti the Teacher

Our wonderful Oldenburg helped Gianna by giving her the confidence she needed to transfer her new knowledge to Selma. When she asked for something correctly, he showed her how well she'd done it with his quick responses. He told her she rode beautifully, and showed her she was strong. Horses not only bring people together, they can teach us, encourage us, and give us strength.

Freedom as a Gift

In addition to riding, Gianna had a second teacher: Socio, our liberty work schoolmaster. Socio's job was to teach her about communication, expressive behavior, and attentiveness. Since the sand was a bit heavy for her to push her wheelchair through, we practiced these conversations on the farm grounds. Gianna's positive attitude helped her learn the signals in no time at all, and Socio provided great feedback. He wasn't concerned at all about the wheelchair, since I had used one myself for a while during training after my own riding accident. Careful, kind exposure can help horses get used to all kinds of situations.

A working conversation has no boundaries—it connects one heart to another.

Never give up. Not only is the glass half full, it's a wonderful glass.

The attentiveness with which Socio approached a complete stranger was so touching. Although it was impressive how clearly Gianna used language—it took only a few minutes for them to find common ground—horses that have learned to listen are simply good at it. This can make life with them so easy and happy.

Never Give Up

Gianna is just getting started. The bond she has with horses gives her strength. She says she can forget she needs to manage without legs when she sits on a horse. Since subtle language is her only means of communication, convincing the horse is her starting point; she can't control him with force or strength. I can't predict when she'll be able to mount Selma independently, but she has time, she has learned to wait, and—most importantly—she never gives up. For her, the glass isn't just half full, it's a wonderful glass.

SELMA AND GIANNA

Team:
Selma, ten-year-old Westfalian mare
Gianna, dressage para rider

Expressive behavior:
Tight, closed mouth; some blinking; swishing tail; defensive

Communication issues:
- active offers but without comprehension of the full task
- lacking spatial awareness: giving and requesting space

Training path:
- Learn to read horse's expressive behavior and react appropriately
- Learn communication, expressive behavior and track
- Strengthen trust
- Take time, allow time

IT'S NEVER TOO LATE

The time we invest in training our animals can feel like time lost or time well-spent, depending on how we use it. If we don't have a good plan and keep making the same mistakes or getting stuck on the same topic, then the time spent can seem costly. I don't know anyone who hasn't, at one time or another, found themselves revisiting the same problem, stuck on a training issue like it's a knot that won't untangle.

WHEN THE HORSE MAKES THE RULES

You need to develop the ability to answer your own questions in order to be able to successfully communicate with your horse. The ability to objectively read expressive behavior is one important part of the equation, and the use of a very clear communication system is the other. The benchmark we must always return to is good listening and clear speaking. Reading this, you may think that sounds far too simple, but the reality is that it really should be that clear-cut. The difficulty lies in our own perceptions, our feelings, our ambition, and our anger or helplessness.

For some horse and rider pairs, years go by without anything seeming to change in their relationship. Sometimes people think it's too late; the horse is too old, or the problems are too ingrained. Perhaps either horse or rider may struggle to find the motivation. But keep in mind: there's no such thing as too old, too late, or too lazy when it comes to learning to communicate better. There is only one thing to do: get started. Horses are always ready to go back to the beginning. (We saw that with Hermann.) They are always willing to make a fresh start—to be a blank slate for us. It's up to us to write something new; if we don't, we shouldn't be surprised if we keep getting the same response.

LEARNING FROM EXPERIENCE

Filou was a macho horse through and through—an approved breeding stallion that, by the age of 19, had a few very bad habits that made it difficult to handle him. When his hormones got the better of him, he didn't hesitate to bite his handler, rear up and strike out with his front hooves, or threaten people by crowding them or swinging his haunches into their space. He made his own rules. Since gelding an older horse isn't recommended, when Maureen got Filou at age 18, she decided to look for other options. That's when he and I met.

Inside, They're All the Same

Filou was gorgeous. He had an impressive presence. It didn't matter that he was a mini Shetland. What he lacked in size, he made up for with charisma. He was a premium stallion, a pinto in a class of his own. But he was stiff from front to back, looking tight and awkward when he moved.

Filou was out of shape and rude. The first thing Maureen needed to do was define her personal space and teach him to respect it. Filou was completely uninhibited and desperately needed rules to follow.

Rule number one: he simply wasn't allowed to get close to her. Filou's functional pattern of aggressiveness was so extremely over-developed that, regardless of the question he was asked, his response would be, "I can bite you or I can kick you—you decide!" or "Get out of my way, here I come!" It was hard work to teach him boundaries and spatial awareness. We practiced in short bursts, because his ability to concentrate was limited. He was only "online" for short periods of time before he began to get overwhelmed and we would lose his attention again. We mixed a bit of longeing in with leading, and as soon as he found the right answer to a question—for example, giving Maureen the space she had asked for—we let him trot in a small circle.

Every time he got too close to Maureen, she said in a kind tone, "Hey, hey," and started to push him back out with assertive body language. Maureen imagined her defensive zone as a hula hoop floating around her middle, and that way, she could easily tell when Filou invaded her space. She maintained her space by refusing to let Filou move her; she held her ground and demanded that he stay out of the space around her body. After confirming she could maintain her space while standing still, we also started working on this at the walk. It took three sessions, and four months total, until the rules regarding proximity and distance were established and Filou understood how to follow them.

Sharing adventures and having fun can pave the way for successful training.

Gaining the horse's attention is the first step.

Productive training sessions are the result of successful dialogue.

Choosing a Starting Point

We decided to establish boundaries as the first pillar, because Filou's massive—and, in part, defensive—pushiness and lack of respect for space made it impossible to address responsiveness or rewardability. It took a very deliberate introduction of mutual respect before Maureen could become his coach.

It became apparent that Filou had no idea what his real name was. Up to this point, he seemed to think his name was "No." So, after establishing boundaries, we began to school the next pillar: responsiveness to his name. Maureen stood next to her stallion and said his name—no reaction. She said in a friendly tone, "Come," because he knew that already from our work on giving and requesting space. This time, the ear closer to her focused on her. She said his name again, as if praising him.

To clarify the principle of rewardability for him, we started to give him space instead of solely focusing on holding or defending boundaries, or requesting space (as we had up until now). Maureen also learned to reliably find his favorite scratching spots. For these two, practicing rewardability was a bit of a balancing act, because it often resulted in Filou getting pushy. He had to learn that, when Maureen praised him, it didn't mean he could bite her or take the opportunity to rear. That was the rule: The handler can enter a horse's personal space, but the horse can't barge into hers. Somehow we had to get this into his pretty head, so we kept asking him to keep his distance, and kept praising him for good behavior.

Building Their House—One Pillar at a Time

Maureen practiced hard. She worked on the four pillars and schooled the three elements of each one: Filou's answers had to be prompt, friendly, and correct. She longed Filou and went for walks with him, and they started to enjoy these adventures together. Filou's body changed; he became slimmer and more muscular. In about six months, Maureen had fully developed all four pillars and the three elements of each. She now had a sturdy foundation, and we were ready to start adding gymnastic exercise.

For some horses, it takes a while to reawaken their innate desire to bond. It's important not to lose your sense of humor.

Gymnastic Training for the Macho Man

It had been important for us to be able to teach this little man rules and help him build strength before we moved forward with his training, but that day had finally arrived. We followed the training scale (Rhythm, Relaxation, Connection, Impulsion, Straightness, and Collection) while we worked with him on the ground; the lessons build on each other there just as they do under saddle. It's important to follow this system of correct gymnastic training—be careful to not just teach anything that comes to mind. Gymnastic training is progressive.

Logically and Systematically

Each lesson taught is a logical progression in a series. After the horse understands leading on the track, we begin to teach him to bow, and then on to kneeling. From there, we teach lying down, then lying flat, and lastly sitting. All these lessons are built on the principle of "active offers," which means when I close one door, my four-legged partner should search confidently and calmly for another door that is open. When you work with your horse, make sure this is exactly what happens. If he starts looking or begging for treats, loses balance, or begins to act stressed, try to correct his inner attitude; slow the training and work on:

— rewardability
— responsiveness
— attention-shifting
— acceptance of the aids

This way, your horse won't just hectically sprint through lessons, but rather will truly learn and will perform the tasks asked of him joyfully. Filou made sure we worked slowly with him. If we didn't, he would become frantic, tossing his head and dancing around on his little legs at top speed. But the more calmly Maureen worked, the more clearly she managed the space, and the more steadfast she became, the easier it was for the little stallion to concentrate and cooperate.

Big Little Personality

It's often the same for small horses as it is for small dogs: People don't tend to take them seriously, and rather than spend time training them, owners often just handle them physically and correct them with force. This alone can make small horses turn grumpy and show defensive behavior. Look at it this way: if your horse pulls his head away—for example, to graze—do you pull on the lead and yank your horse's head up? If so, what could you do better? Learn to defend your space without giving in, but don't pull back either.

Remember your four tools. First, responsiveness: address your horse by his name. Try, even if you think it won't work, to redirect your horse's attention. And if these efforts truly fail, then hold your space and start to emphasize your request. First, use the warning signal of "Come," or "Hey." Then tap the end of the lead against your own jacket for as long as it takes, with as much intensity as you need to interrupt your horse's behavior so he starts to pay attention to you. Now repeat his name, give him space, and praise him until the praise works. This approach (see page 31) works without force, without punishment, and without yelling. It develops respect and trust in equal measure.

To Persuade, Not Overpower

We were very careful, with our little macho man, not to let force come into play. Maureen wanted to persuade him, not overpower him. It paid off: after one year of training, she bought a sulky. Before introducing him to driving, she began with training at liberty and led him alongside her while she rode a bike. She specifically focused on improving his fitness, his happiness, and his sociability.

Winning the Jackpot

Maureen took a gamble when she took on Filou, but it paid off. She started with an old, grumpy, shaggy former breeding stallion with no muscling and plenty of bad habits, and changed him into an exemplary partner. She has, like many of our students, proven it's never too late to start on the right path.

FILOU AND MAUREEN

Team:

Filou, 20-year-old mini Shetland stallion

Maureen, madly in love with her horse

Expressive behavior:

Tight in his whole body

Communication issues:

- lack of boundaries
- aggressive and pushy
- lacking physical fitness, limited ability to concentrate

Training path:

- Learn to read expressive behavior and react appropriately
- Define, recognize, and maintain space
- Basic training on the four pillars and three elements of each
- Define use of space; establish rules and boundaries
- Train comfort zones while maintaining space
- Leading, communicative longeing, going for walks, leading from a bike for fitness
- Work in hand and in liberty, bowing and laying down

TRAINING WITH ME: BERTI

My system isn't just for schooling horses. We've discussed the four pillars and the three elements of the horse's response in depth, how to read the horse's expressive behavior, and how to objectively listen to him. There are six functional patterns into which we sorted behavior, and you can now decide whether your horse needs more comfort zone training and more or less space. My system is not only safe, it also virtually guarantees success for you and for your horse.

BE THEIR FAVORITE PERSON

It's all about trust, real bonding, and a deep connection to your horse, always. Often, misunderstandings arise simply because people rush through training too quickly, we're too superficial in how we communicate, and we become too harsh when we feel helpless or frustrated. We all want to be our horse's favorite person. We also want to please our horse, and we want to do everything right. We want to be our best selves, the best team, and—of course—give our best performance. You have learned that:

- it's the bond you build that makes you strong as a team and helps the horse manage stress
- it's clear and consistent language that eliminates misunderstandings
- it's the right amount of physical exertion that creates happiness.

How often do people want to do everything right with their horse from the start, and how often do they only succeed some of the time?

THE RIGHT HORSE FOR THE JOB... PERHAPS

"Black, may turn white." Jan, my husband, had the tablet in his hand and sat down next to me by the bed. It was actually too early to think clearly. I'll never understand why my husband leaves bed at 5 o'clock in the morning to browse through horse ads, but this time, he got my attention. The ad was for a Westphalian foal with a wonderful pedigree. It was still too early for more than one syllable from me in response, though: "Where?"

That very evening, we found ourselves at a beautiful breeding facility. I had a clear goal in mind: this horse would be for competing in dressage. His eyes, his expression, and his gaits promised it. I fell in love with him. He was alert, fresh, but gentle and trusting at the same time. This seemed to be the perfect horse to have by my side, and everyone there agreed with me.

BEST OF...BERTI!

We brought him home in the fall, and named him "Best of Krüger-Degener," but he kept his nickname of Berti. After he got to know our Lusitano Socio, who always takes care of new arrivals, both went out to pasture together.

But Berti trotted off looking like a Bernese Mountain Dog. His tail was curled up over his tense back, and he held his head very high. He wasn't blinking, and looked like he was barely breathing. This full-body tension would turn out to be a regular problem.

BERTIE TURNS TWO

Berti took a really long time to grow. He still needed one more year to develop before he'd be ready to start under saddle. We used this time to prepare him for riding; by the time he turned two, we had confirmed the skills he'd learned on the ground—leading, bowing, laying down, and longeing (both communicative and classical). He was—and still is—very easily distracted by external stimuli, and he has an incredibly quick reaction time.

Although he spent most of his time in the pasture with his buddies, his sensitivity to his environment presented a constant challenge when we needed to handle him. An umbrella, an unusually parked wheelbarrow, or a dog zooming around the corner could make him tense. I had to work hard to keep his focus on me. Most of the time I succeeded by working on responsiveness. I sometimes had to be very clear about requesting space so I could slow him down and maintain my boundaries. It was becoming clear to me that if I wanted to win this horse over, he would need structure: calm, consistency, and plenty of safe space.

When Berti acted naughty, I know he didn't mean to annoy me, but he still sometimes managed to frustrate me enormously. I realized the balance between criticism and praise was quickly beginning to tip toward criticism, so I embarked on strengthening his desire to bond. I worked intensively with him on training rewardability. I took every possible opportunity to spend time with him in the pasture or in his stall, or I'd walk into the arena with him, just to look for his favorite scratching spots.

As a two-year-old, Berti already knew how to lie down. It's a good idea to teach this skill in order to prepare young horses for other lessons later in life.

BERTI TURNS THREE

The four pillars were confirmed: at three, Berti could lead, longe, bow, load, and lie down. We were slowly but surely getting to the point where we could start thinking about work under saddle. Here, Berti was uncomplicated and trusted me very much, which was thanks in no small part to good genes, but also to our thorough preparation up to this point. Unfortunately, he struggled with the canter. He kept changing behind, and he lost his balance each time this happened. He still needed more time and strength. In addition to being a bit uncoordinated, he was only slightly taller than 16 hands, and I was afraid that my Berti would be too small for me.

Tension continued to be a problem; the quality of his walk was affected by how tightly he held his back. It was no small feat to loosen him up while riding. Creating a soft contact while riding him was similarly very difficult. If there were any external stressors, he would get tight in the mouth, grab the bit, and just speed off.

I wasn't at all sure I would be able to achieve my goals with this horse. Yes, he was handsome, but the constant tension was a real problem. I decided to ignore my doubts for another year and forge ahead. We took him with us to a lot of events. At one show, we had temporary stabling on grass. While left to his own devices in his stall, Berti decided to dig, and he didn't rest until he'd dug a hole several feet deep. Berti could squeal and scream like no other horse when he wasn't the first horse brought into the barn. He would jump into the air on all fours and spin around as he did so, followed by flinging his head up and kicking in all directions. It seemed aggressive, almost like rage, but it was a mystery as to who he was so mad at. The energy this horse had was indescribable; it was getting harder and harder to ignore my doubts.

Working at liberty is a wonderful enrichment activity in a partnership.

POWER IS MEANINGLESS WHEN CONTROL IS ABSENT

I kept all this in mind during my daily training with him. I started to work him in the water and trained him to accept my leading him while riding a bike. I was looking for ways to help him coordinate his power, release it in a controlled way, and use his body properly. Berti was becoming a pro at liberty work with me on the ground and on the bike.

This relaxed work, always thinking about sending his energy forward, combined with water training, turned out to be the key to resolving his anger and reining in his power.

We spent plenty of time riding out into the countryside; we started to climb up hills and go on great adventures together. It seemed like Berti was beginning to trust me. Cross-country, he was a dream: powerful, dynamic, and always forward. As long as we didn't run into any trouble, he did a good job. It was only the first few steps that were difficult, because he had to work through his high tension first.

AN OUTSIDE PERSPECTIVE

"He has to go where you send him!" Johannes said to me again and again. He has been my trainer for over ten years, and he breeds and trains his horses from start to finish. He has a good eye, excellent feel, and lots of knowledge, and he teaches well. I need this outside perspective once in a while. Having people around you who understand both you and the horse is an indispensable part of training. This is also why Carla and I often switch roles. No one knows me, my philosophy, and my horses as well as she does; her feedback is so valuable. Everyone needs eyes on the ground at least occasionally. If you can't find anyone with the necessary skills to help, then just let yourself be filmed. Whether you work your horses in-hand or under saddle, an outside perspective brings objectivity and honesty into the dialogue between you and your horse.

The development of spatial language stayed part of our daily warm-up training.

VARIETY IS THE SPICE OF LIFE

It was the right decision to introduce my Berti to a diverse array of training approaches, since smart, ambitious horses need to keep their minds as well as their bodies busy. Sadly, however, broadening his horizons didn't help him understand that the odd umbrella wasn't going to be the end of him. No, he had to be threatened by the umbrella every time, and it needed to be investigated every time to make sure it was not going to eat him, and often several more times in the same session. His favorite thing to hate was corners: he would get tense, and while kicking off, he would hurl sand against the boards. That, of course, caused a rattling sound, which became yet another reason for him to consider corners a threat. Since we ride in a rectangular arena, these corners are part of our dressage life. He truly tested my patience—but the moment I accepted his behavior with humor, it got better.

This was an issue where he constantly tested me. Not me personally, but the aids I needed to support the signals I gave him.

He quickly grasped the nuances of my signals, but he was constantly looking for a way to get off track. He tested outside as well as inside aids. The same qualities that

Establishing a mutual dialogue and experiencing harmony...

...while working together should be a part of every experience with a horse.

made him so splendid and so energetic also caused him to be aggressive. It was up to me to close the right doors early enough, to be faster than him—and do it without emotion, because if I got as angry as he did, we would spend all our time fighting, and I would surely lose.

With the other horses, Berti was always the one who drove the others in front of him, turned them, and encouraged them. Maybe he was dominant, cunning, or just plain clever, but he was never dishonest. His breeder bred wonderful, honest horses—this one was just too smart for his own good.

BERTI TURNS FOUR

Berti was now four, and he surprised us with another growth spurt. Because he always looked balanced and harmonious, and had never really had a "gawky" phase, he always seemed to be done growing. Between the ages of four and five, however, he gained another two and a half inches. It was clear this horse had a lot of growing pains to deal with, in addition to his excess energy.

CREATING GOALS

I slowed down his training and moved the goal posts as much as I needed to, but soon we were ready to begin competing. We took the time to show him the grounds the day before his first competition, and it became clear very quickly that I wouldn't be able to just "saddle up and go" with him. He simply needed time to deal with his adrenaline.

The feeling in the test, however, was lovely. Even with his baseline tension, he carried himself and me powerfully and easily through the test, and he listened to me the entire time. During this adventure, I discovered I could truly rely on him.

Patience is the most important lesson in life.

Being a horse's safe place means he will always seek out your company. This kind of partnership contains freedom, bonding, and happiness in equal measure.

I think this horse came into my life to teach me a very important lesson: patience. I thought I was already a patient person, but he showed me I needed and was capable of finding far more patience than ever before.

BERTI TURNS FIVE

Berti was really good working at liberty, but he always kept just a bit too much distance from me. Attention-shifting was well established; with a very quiet, "Hey, hey," I could easily redirect him. Lying down, lying down flat, and sitting were solid, and bicycling together was our favorite thing to do. However, he was still very reactive to the outside world.

Long and low without falling on the forehand, slowing down, waiting—those became the themes during our rides together. He needed to do all this, but still stay in front of my leg; we calmly developed the walk while I asked him to open his poll and reach forward with his neck. He would habitually curl up and keep his already short neck very tight. I kept working on lengthening his neck, developing acceptance of the bit, and maintaining the regularity of his footfalls. His walk in particular needed much more relaxation. Meanwhile, the extended paces and counter canter were solid. When I did everything correctly and Berti carried himself well, the strength in his movement, his balance, and his forward energy captivated me. In these moments, I absolutely understood the German saying, "True happiness is found on the backs of horses."

He was so strong, rhythmic, and dynamic that I forgot all our troubles—we worked as one. These moments kept me going. We continued to compete, and we placed well every time. I did sense, though, that he still lacked strength. While he looked like a body builder, apparently he still needed more fitness.

BERTI TURNS SIX

"He'll never be able to do this!" I complained, because we were absolutely stuck on flying changes. He would change late behind instead of jumping through back to front, and, even worse, he got hot, running through the half-halt to change ahead of and against my aids. This set us way back in his training.

I pictured our control knobs for tempo, energy, and difficulty, and turned down the tempo and energy, but made difficult work a priority in his training. I kept our warm-up short, then moved right into rigorous work. We still couldn't get the changes. I abandoned flying changes temporarily, and began to introduce half steps, since I thought maybe he needed to become quicker and stronger behind. Working on them from the ground, I got the same response from him: "I'm going to push away, and you're going to leave me alone!" So I reduced my training goals and became calmer, and he began to understand what I was asking. He stepped correctly with a diagonal pair once—praise until the praise works. Then he did it twice. Suddenly, he was working with me.

Now I transferred his new-found ability to perform half steps to those flying changes. Learning half steps had taught him to lower his croup a little and begin to carry more weight on his haunches. This countered his natural inclination to catapult his croup into the air whenever something provoked him. Learning this new response not only helped Berti with his changes, it transformed how he understood his ridden work. From that moment on, progress came quickly.

RELAXED HUMAN = RELAXED HORSE

Suddenly it was obvious: I had been driven by ambition. I had allowed myself to be motivated only by my own goals, and had been blind to what Berti truly needed in his current situation. Because I had been so focused on nailing a correct flying change (and then the next thing, and the next...), I had stopped working on bonding. I felt terrible. From that point on, we spent more time working on rewardability and on the little games we used to play together.

I focused on making rewardability an important element in our training, and Berti thrived with this new routine. This doesn't mean I just stood there constantly praising him—but I did spend considerably more time on social grooming behavior. Aside from that, I spent at least two-thirds of our training time focusing on relaxation: we spent plenty of time riding long and low at the walk and trot on gentle lines. I used this time to address Berti's obedience to the leg and relaxation in the poll. Once I was sure he was active and balanced, I'd give him another walk break. This was followed with a long canter set where I focused on alternating between extension and collection, simple changes, counter canter, and voltes. I would only ask for flying changes when his canter was engaged and his poll relaxed.

Berti seemed to think of himself as quick and reactive—a sporty Porsche—but in reality he was more like a diesel engine. It took him a long time to warm up, but once he was ready, his mind and his body matched better. Once I took the time to really know him, he was able to show me what he needed in order to succeed, and I in turn was able to take this knowledge to heart as we worked together.

Remember Violetta? She worked best the exact opposite way: she did her best work at the beginning of a ride. The more she warmed up, the quicker she made mistakes. With her, too, we had to develop a very indi-

Only if we are humble can we act in the horse's best interest.

Training that looks easy often consists of steps that are no longer visible.

vidualized warm-up, because it was clear we had to do the difficult things right after she was warmed up. Find out what type of warm-up routine works best for your horse. Work in intervals, watch the time, and document your observations. Build in rituals that are good for body and mind, listen to your horse, and learn his preferences so you can incorporate them into his training.

MY BERTI

He's one of a kind, a real character, beautiful and incredibly strong. He challenges me on every level. When I stand in front of him and look at him, I get the feeling I really want to be his favorite human. I also want to be his friend and his safe place. He has taught me so much: to wait, to find innovative ways to reach a goal, to allow for detours, to be quieter and clearer. He has proven I'm right in never meeting aggression with force, and yet he caused me to constantly question myself, and in doing so he made me take a closer look at our work together and re-commit to my system of training in harmony.

COURAGE

Where do you stand in your own efforts to become a builder of happiness and harmony? Which questions have caused you to re-evaluate something? Which expressive behaviors and dynamics have dominated your training? With this book, I hope to raise awareness about the importance of dialogue and encourage you to think about these questions. Every single horse is an individual piece of art, art that only becomes more beautiful when his trainer is diligent in training with competence and empathy. Self-doubt is part of this. Have the courage to be comfortable with being creative, taking detours, setting limits, and—above all—being willing to change your point of view.

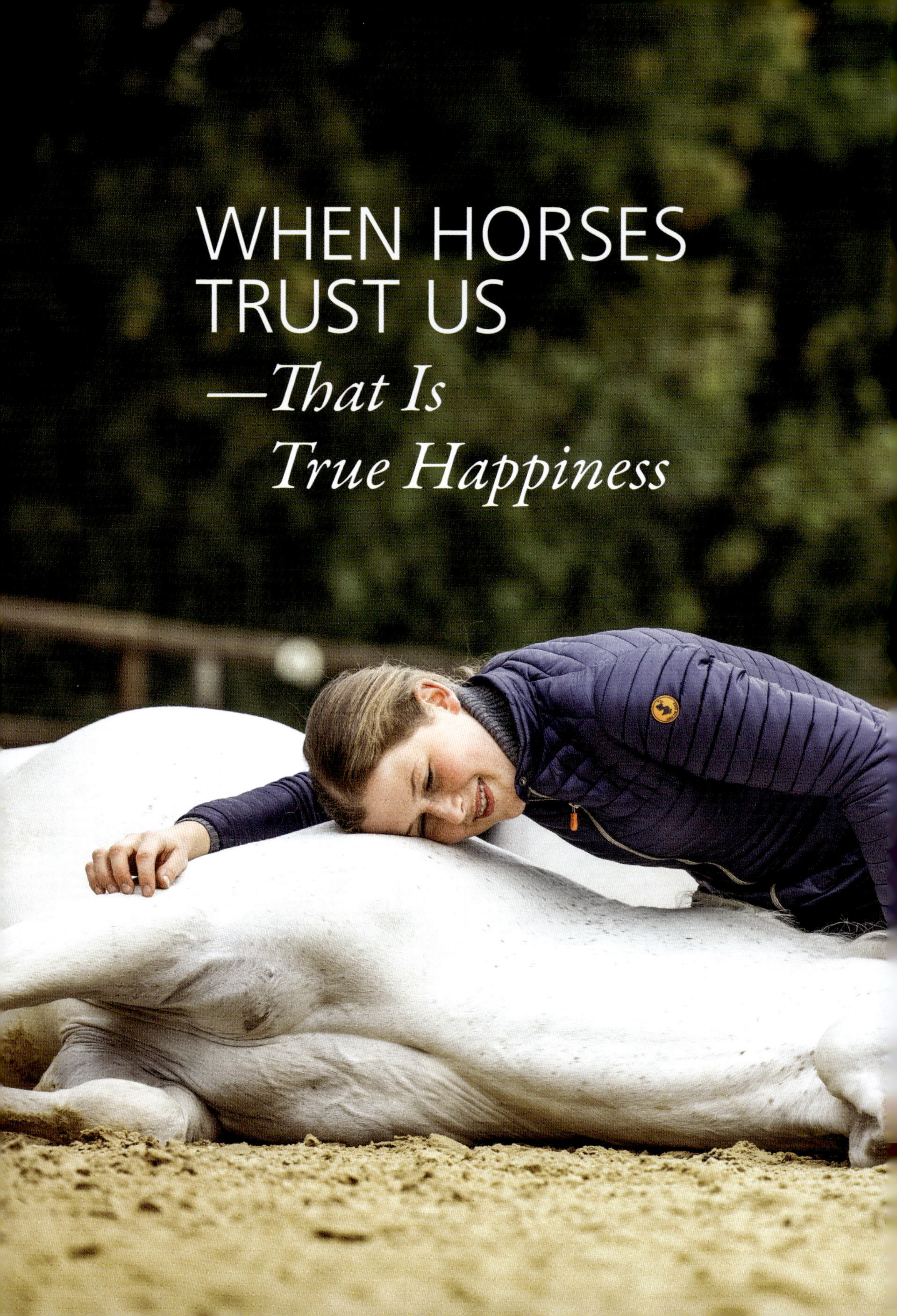
WHEN HORSES
TRUST US
—That Is
True Happiness

uvex

IN HARMONY WITH THE HORSE

It sounds so nice: being in harmony with the horse, in unison ... but let's take an honest look at this idea. Many things in the life of a horse happen to him entirely without his consent. Given a choice, he would never agree to plenty of what is asked of him. No foal voluntarily lets himself be tied, goes to the farrier, or leaves his mother (or his family, his herd) to go, free and unburdened, to a new owner. Nor would he ask to be ridden or driven. Observed objectively, horses are often forced to enter into work for a human. It doesn't matter to the horse whether it's for leisure, sport, or business. We don't have to sugarcoat it. But what we should do is understand what submission means for a horse, and think carefully about how we go about getting it. The expressive behavior of a horse makes it easy to recognize when we definitely *don't* have his consent. Most often, this manifests as tension, blockages, or bouts of anger. Horses deal with stress by blocking it off, and by getting tight or aggressive (either offensively or defensively—it doesn't matter which). These are cries for help from horses that are stressed, can't tell you where it hurts, and are quietly unhappy.

By now, you have learned to observe your horse closely. You have learned to read his behaviors and expressions and listen to him. This is exactly where my system starts: It teaches you to look more closely, and to recognize the signals your horse is giving you before anger develops. Training in harmony means slowing down the dialogue and having deeper discussions.

As an apprentice in my system of training, you should not only be able to read what's there, but also be able to see what's missing. Cues that you might once have easily missed are now clear, and in this new and intimate space, you can engage in a genuine dialogue with your horse.

Quietly and gently, horse and rider take care of each other.

STRESS-FREE LOADING

Let's look at how to apply my system to a common activity that can also be stressful: loading onto a trailer. We'll discuss the horse's perspective, the application of three-dimensional language, and how to obtain consent.

CONFIDENCE CREATES SUCCESS

There are people who break out in a sweat just thinking about having to load their horse. There are also horses that refuse to even be haltered when they see the trailer arriving. Aside from the fact that loading might become necessary to save your horse's life if he ever needs an emergency vet visit, loading should be part of basic education for horses.

For a horse, there is no reason to ever want to enter a cramped, loud, unsteady box from which he can't escape. Prey animals always need to be able to see a possible escape route so their fight-or-flight response isn't triggered. Being separated from his friends in a dark box, like a trailer, essentially represents the epitome of a threat—a horse's instinctual drive for survival will understandably kick in. This is one of many situations in a horse's life where it simply makes no sense for him to cooperate, from his perspective. We have to find a way to help him cope with this situation that works with instead of against his naturally linear way of thinking. Ideally, he will recognize that walking into the trailer is a solution, an answer to a question, and he'll see the trailer as a place of comfort. In the best-case scenario, loading becomes his own idea, which decreases the stress of it significantly.

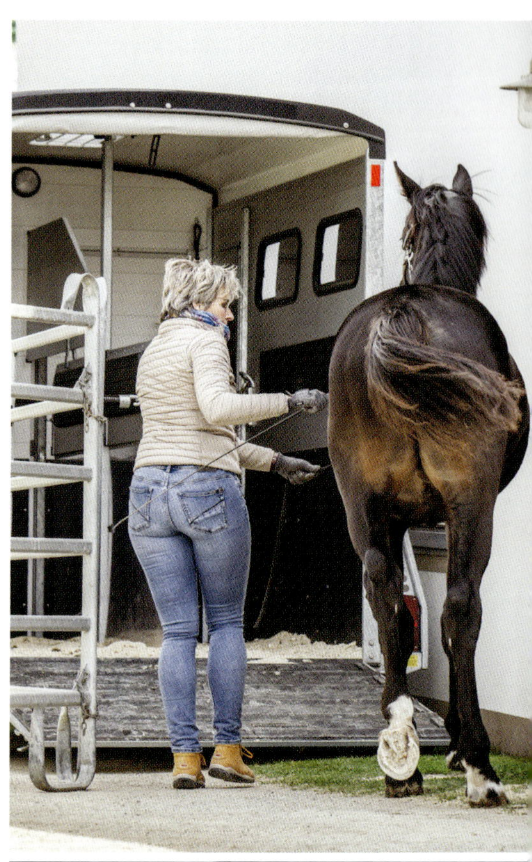

Loading should become the horse's idea.

SET UP FOR SUCCESS

Park your trailer on a level spot next to a building and turn the motor off. Place a barrier (like the fencing panels shown here) on the open side of the trailer, and attach another one to the end of the first so you can use it as a small enclosure. Wear safe shoes, remove your spurs, use gloves, and protect your horse's legs with bandages or boots. Make sure your horse is wearing a well-fitting halter. Make sure your horse fully understands the first step needed before you train a horse to load—leading correctly—before you try to go any farther. While learning to lead, he'll have already learned the three methods of communication we use for training (page 48) and he'll understand that his handler always walks next to his shoulder. In addition, he'll already understand the concept of rewardability and establishing boundaries, and will know how to handle a situation where his trainer might maintain her space, ask for more space, and so on. Your prior work on rewardability ensures he already knows he can relax, and he also knows how to respond to acoustic signals that tell him to move forward. You can see here the importance and usefulness of the basics.

Make sure you have a second person to assist you, and do what you can to limit additional stressors or distractions like passing cars, kids playing nearby, or dogs running around. Create a quiet, safe learning environment for your horse to set him up for success. Also, make sure you have plenty of time to work on this, because you may need it.

FROM THE HORSE'S POINT OF VIEW

Bring your horse calmly into the pre-loading area. Slowly close that area with the gate you've set up, and give your horse time to assess the situation. Hold your space and your

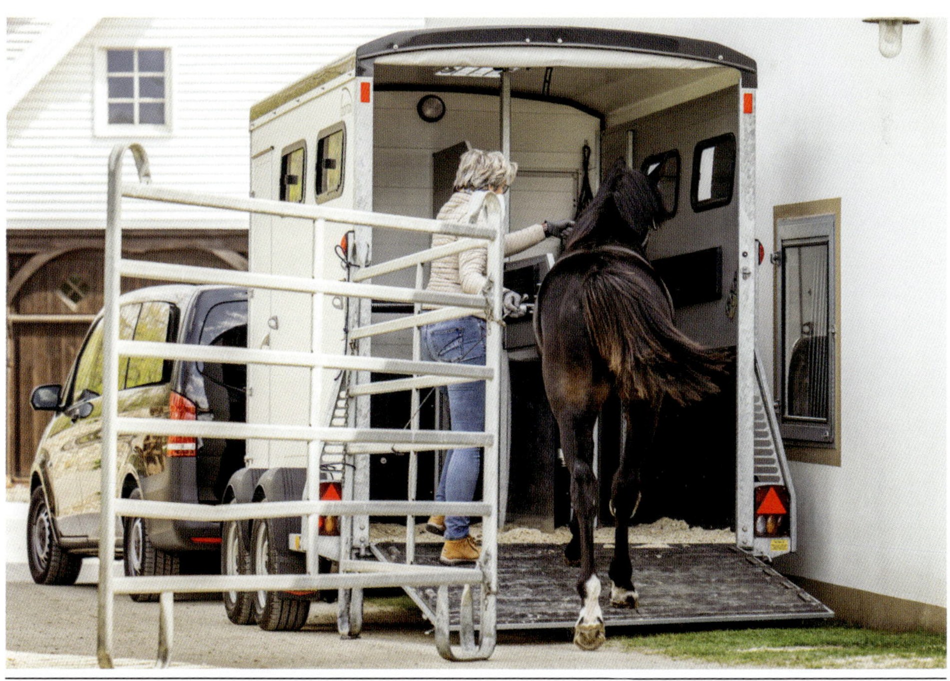

Here we need direction, space, rules, motivation, safety, and comfort—but never any pressure.

In a calm environment, your horse can learn to decide for himself to choose the right path.

path, and don't let your horse turn away from the trailer.

Give your horse as much time as he needs to see everything, and start with praise. You can't expect a correct response immediately, but praise and comfort him regardless. Your most important job is to calmly keep his focus aimed in the right direction, and to hold your space while positioning your horse's head toward the trailer. Training a horse to load works best when you stay calm and unambitious. You shouldn't plan to get your horse in the trailer on your first attempt. Instead, your goal should be to quietly work on the four pillars of my system, even in situations like this. Only then can you provide security and support to your horse. Be understanding when your horse feels stressed, and continue to work on bonding.

When you observe your horse, you might see the following: maybe he isn't blinking, is holding his breath, is pressing his lips together, or is holding his head very high; maybe his back is tense, his ears are back, and the underside of his neck is tight. Give yourself and his sympathetic nervous system time to process the situation at hand. The horse is now becoming aware of the limits of the space he is in and is assessing his possible escape routes. Because all the other doors are closed, the only available open door is the entrance into the trailer, but he hasn't yet come to terms with that.

RESPECT AND TRUST

The balance between the most important components of animal training, namely respect and trust, is crucial. To maintain respect, you need to hold your space. Sometimes it's not easy to prevent a horse from turning around when he wants to.

He has to respect his handler's space; he isn't allowed to push into her space, just like he wouldn't be allowed to push anoth-

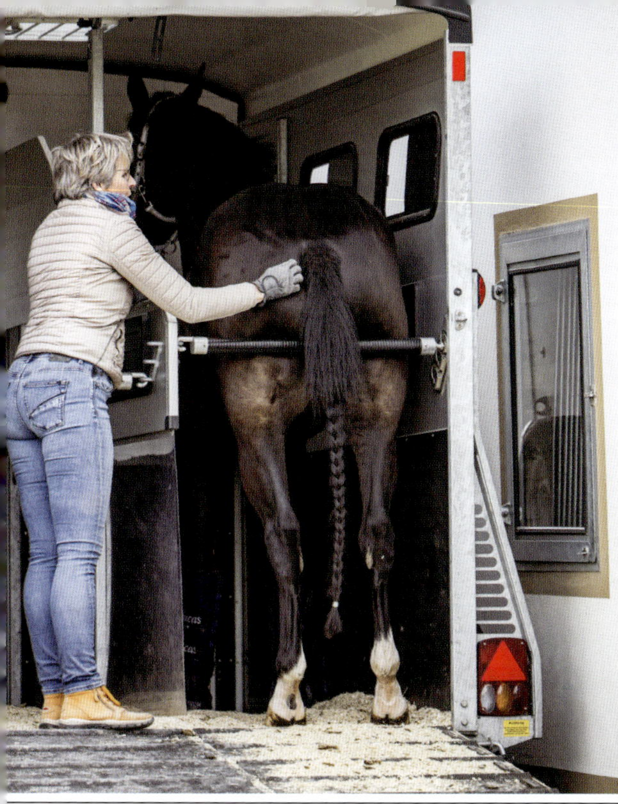

Practice calmly and without pressure.

er horse aside. At the same time, he isn't allowed to pull away, and he has to accept the physical boundaries of the situation. On the other hand, he needs to trust his handler: this is what keeps him willing to communicate, gives him security, and allows him to find comfort.

In a situation where I realize that neither trust nor respect are present, teaching that would be my first and possibly only job. As an apprentice in my system, you should always keep in mind that we have to work first on the *how*, followed by the *what*. Ask yourself whether you want to just load your horse as quickly as possible, or focus on a lasting lesson that prioritizes the balance between respect and trust.

HIS OWN IDEA

You have now created a setting with a secure "outside," and you represent a soft and safe "inside" to your horse. Consider the basic framework of bonding (page 88); your horse will find the solution himself once you focus on engaging in a linear dialogue with him instead of worrying about the complexity of loading. Usually, it's the other way around: Someone wants to load the horse, there are no boundaries around the trailer (the "outside" isn't defined or secure), and the human trying to load the horse (the "inside") is tense instead of reassuring or comforting. Why would the horse want to consent to something like walking into a trailer? If you want your horse to feel like it's his idea to enter the trailer, then you have to allow him the opportunity to come up with this idea in his own time. Once he's thought of it himself, loading can be a reliably stress-free experience.

PLAN BETTER THAN A HORSE

Ideally, you should be able to send your horse into the trailer while you stand next to the ramp, asking him to enter and stand still until you have secured the butt bar. This is always the safest and most comfortable way to load. It works as long as you can close other possible escape routes before your horse sees them, and have a clear "open door" that leads into the trailer.

THE DIALOGUE

At this moment, you're still standing in the pre-loading area with your horse. Start to read his expressive behavior—take your time. Notice his mouth, his breathing, and his nostrils, eyes, and ears. Can you tell where he's looking? Is he focused on the trailer, or is he looking somewhere else? Behind himself?

If he's looking backward, don't ask any other questions. Wait and praise him. Create a comfort zone and let him know he has time—there's never any hurry. If he shows any interest in the trailer, leave him to it, but do not, under any circumstances, let him turn around. He must stay in the space next to you—no ifs, ands, or buts! Watch his eyes. Only when he's blinking and calm, and his gaze is directed in front of him, should you start asking him to walk on.

THE HORSE HAS TO CHOOSE

Usually, a horse will take a step or two, but as soon as he approaches the loading ramp, everything stops: no movement, breathing, or blinking. Which means we wait again.

Your horse may think about choosing to listen to his flight instincts—which means he will go not forward, but behind him, turning toward where he thinks an escape route might be. Only when he realizes this path is closed off will he redirect his focus forward again. You should make every effort to stand calmly next to him, looking into and turned toward the trailer. As slow as this process may seem, in reality it will save a lot of time and avoid a lot of stress. You aren't standing there doing nothing; you're having a calm, clear dialogue with your horse and teaching him acceptance. The alternative is to spend hour after hour fighting with your horse and walking in circles, scolding him and probably cursing at least a little, and, in the end, needing to get someone else to help anyway. The only benefit to that approach is the exercise you'll get while you walk in circles—and while you're doing that, you're also teaching your horse that he can avoid the trailer and that he's stronger than you.

INTELLIGENCE AND COMMUNICATION INSTEAD OF POWER STRUGGLES

Now your horse has put one foot on the loading ramp. This is reason enough to lavishly praise him, even if he immediately steps backward again. Stay at his shoulder, with no particular plans, relaxed and calm. Horses gain more confidence in the loading process when they're allowed to walk backward if they try to, and there's no point trying to prevent it. You can stay relaxed; he can't go anywhere, after all, because you set up those pre-loading barriers. In most cases, it takes about three to seven minutes before the horse is calm enough to trust you and find his way into the trailer by himself.

TAKE YOUR TIME

And just like that, your horse's inherent ability to trust wins out over his inherent ability to be wary—what a fantastic moment. Take care, especially with young horses, not to put up the butt bar too quickly. Just wait, and if your horse starts backing out of the trailer, allow it. Always remember: the *how* comes before the *what*. First, just teach him to walk into the trailer; then, as a separate step, you can address how long he stays there.

The more reliably your horse enters the trailer, the easier it will be for him to accept comfort zone training inside the trailer.

Trailer loading is part of the education of a young horse.

It's important to have a safe and successful system...

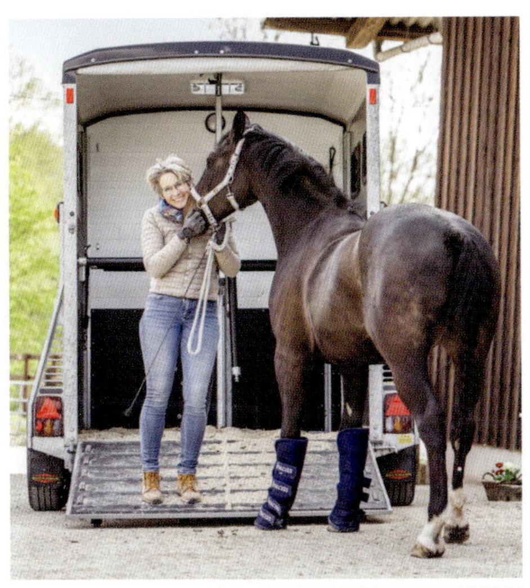

...that includes plenty of praise and affirmation.

If you ask too much of him all at once, he may feel threatened, which means you'll have to start from scratch. Stay calm and focused regardless of the situation. Study his expressive behavior and help him find the solution himself; this is the only way to create a positive experience with a reliable training outcome. Your goal is a safe horse who loads easily and without problems—who considers traveling with you an enjoyable experience and not a threatening one.

ONE STEP AT A TIME

Once you're confident your horse will reliably choose the correct answer in this setting, and he's showing no blockages or tension anywhere, you can remove the back wall of the pre-loading barrier. If you still have no problems, after that you can take away the barrier next to the trailer. If he still enters happily, you can move the trailer to a different location, with no boundaries at all. This way, you're removing the aids one by one and taking small steps to ensure your horse continues to build confidence. It's very likely your horse will start to offer his solutions to you voluntarily. It is a truly sublime feeling when you walk with your horse toward a trailer and it's clear he wants to enter as soon as he sees the opening.

This is just one example of how to obtain a horse's consent. Riding in a trailer is also not something a horse would voluntarily choose to do; it's usually in their best interests that they're back there, but ultimately it's something they're forced to do. Don't be afraid to approach training your horse head-on, but always design every lesson with a successful dialogue in mind. When you master this ability to converse with your horse, you'll be amazed at how many of your ideas a horse can learn to choose for himself.

Being open to a horse's reactions means really seeing them, without judgment.

THE NUANCES OF FUNCTIONAL PATTERNS

With people, misunderstandings can happen within even the healthiest relationships, and here we're talking about individuals who are of the same species, use the same language, and probably have similar life circumstances and histories. With a human partner, it's possible to follow up conflict with a clarifying conversation. If, however, we think about the relationship between a human and their equine partner, the amount of room for misunderstanding is exponentially larger. And an animal can't share his opinion with us after the fact, because he can't bring up earlier arguments and he can't use language to defend himself. As his trainer and partner, you are obligated to listen to your horse carefully, because otherwise you'll miss the signals he's sending.

JUST THE FACTS

There are six distinct functional patterns (page 23), but they rarely manifest in their purest forms. For example, defensiveness can turn into sudden flight, but it may also look like an aversive type of aggressiveness. Another kind of aggressiveness may manifest as affection with no respect for boundaries, which also can quickly transform into shoving, biting, or demanding space.

The way functional patterns combine with each other varies by the individual and by the situation. That is what makes reading a horse so interesting. It would be very straightforward if each functional pattern only existed in one pure form, and was always presented so clearly it would be impossible to miss. Sadly, this isn't the case. Signals, even the most significant and informative ones, can flash past you so quickly you miss them, because they can be so thoroughly mixed in with other behaviors.

Take Fritz, for example (page 71)—this was the horse that stood quietly and seemed calm. When his owner Nathalie gave him a driving aid, she missed the furrowed brow that often appears when a horse's stress hormones are released, preparing him for fight-or-flight. Fritz didn't decide to furrow his brow; his body reacted this way automatically. But Nathalie had no idea how far into defensive expressive behavior Fritz had gone. We were dealing with passive defensiveness with Fritz, which is often interpreted erroneously by humans as laziness. Reading your horse without judgment, and without committing too early to an opinion, allows you to recognize and understand all of the functional patterns your horse expresses.

Threatening behavior is natural. What's important is how we deal with it.

It's human nature to create a story that we feel can explain a behavior, but this is a classic way to create misunderstandings. The following discrepancies are fertile grounds for misunderstandings:

1. Unintentional changes we make in the timing and speed with which we communicate with our animals.
2. Unintentional changes in the way we communicate with our animals (inconsistency in which signals we are using).
3. Our differing perceptions of time (complex vs linear) and our differing perspectives, which will influence our dialogue.

These differences have their charm, but also create hurdles that have to be overcome through dialogue. The advantage of this work is that you can transfer what you've learned to any other species. You want to become a trusted trainer who instills relaxation and happiness? It's not just about mastering the tools of your trade and using them correctly, it's also about learning to correctly assess the material you're working with—your horse's aptitude and level of ability—because only then can you truly do right by your horse.

Experience adventures together with playful consistency.

It's always about working within the correct limits when working with a horse. Praise him enough, set reasonable expectations, and add pressure in moderation. In order to learn how to assess your raw material—the horse you are training—consider what you've learned about functional patterns and reading expressive behavior. You now understand the importance of staying in the present, of knowing how a horse thinks, and of the different methods of communication. These are the tools you'll need to remain factual and objective, and meet your horse where he is, without judgment.

If we learn to listen to our horses when they communicate,

Then we can use the same means of communication with them—a wonderful way to chat.

It's important to recognize that there are genetic predispositions involved in the development of your horse's personality, which are just as important as taking responsibility for the development of individual learning patterns. Knowing this is part of your job as a good trainer. Be mindful: teaching a horse as many tricks as possible or making him perform fantastic feats isn't the point. Protecting him from any and all physical or psychological demands isn't the point, either. You need to:

— find the right horse for the goals you have in mind (or be willing to adjust your goals) and
— develop your horse to his full potential through intelligent, careful, and deliberate support.

Listen so you can understand, not so you can react.

☞ LEARNING TO LISTEN

Although I've gone into some depth and detail already when it comes to the entire holistic process that truly listening to your horse requires, reading expressive behavior is a topic that deserves endless discussion, even for someone truly practiced.

A tightly squeezed mouth, tightened nostrils, unmoving ears, and no blinking: Are we dealing with defensiveness?

A relaxed poll, soft eyes and ears, relaxed nostrils, and soft mouth: A horse paying attention?

Narrow nostrils, ears pushed back 45 degrees, relaxed eyes, and a tight poll: Maybe the beginning of passive defensiveness?

Relaxed mouth, regular breathing, round nostrils, relaxed eyes, and upright ears: Pushy, or making an active offer?

Holding the poll at an angle, head in slanted position, mouth squeezed shut, narrow nostrils, and no blinking: Is this an offensive threat?

Elongated upper lip, shortened lower lip, stretched poll, and relaxed ears: Comfort behavior, or maintaining his own space?

Elongated lower lip, rounded eye, ears at an angle, and open poll: Is this relaxed behavior, or does the horse want to shake?

Long lower lip, shortened upper lip, closed eyes, ears at an angle: Clearly relaxed behavior.

If helplessness, frustration, or disappointment enter into the relationship, then trust and the willingness to bond will be first to suffer for it.

LOVE WON'T SURVIVE DISILLUSIONMENT

Let's think about the first point: you're searching for a horse that matches your goals. Think about the following sentence: "A good horse has no color." Try to believe it in your heart. This is about partnership, happiness, and reaching your personal goals. The horse you choose must be suitable, because only then will you be willing to give him whatever he needs from you. Frustration paralyzes relationships, and love won't survive disillusionment—which will be the inevitable result, if you can't be realistic and objective about your horse.

Be clear with yourself about what your expectations are, write them down, and rank your priorities. Decide what qualities your horse will need to fulfill the job you want him to do, and search for bloodlines that fit the bill. If you don't want to focus on breeding, then search even more carefully (for as long as it takes), and test each horse you find thoroughly. Only then should you be ready and willing to take on responsibility for another creature.

Remember Luca and Socks? A talented girl and a strong young horse—but their relationship was severely strained and damaged by demands from Luca that Socks couldn't meet. Think about the horse, not just yourself; remember that he won't be able to quit his job without your say-so. He can't just tap your shoulder and tell you that he needs better boundaries, or your methods confuse him, or he's overwhelmed, or he isn't being challenged enough. A horse has no choice. He's forced to make the best of the situation he finds himself in. He does this based on his needs and abilities. If he makes a mistake, he isn't doing it to make us angry. Most of the time, he's making choices based on the options he thinks are available to him; sometimes these actions can be frustrating for us, and in the worst-case scenario, they can be dangerous.

With this in mind, make sure your "dream horse" truly matches the goals you have for your equine partner, because every real relationship is like building a house together—for as long as it takes. You, as the trainer, are the architect, and you are designing that house from the ground up. To do this, you need to be able to really see and understand your horse's functional patterns of behavior.

MAKING THE BEST OF IT

Now to the second point: Once you've found your horse (or more than one), it's important to see him as a whole being. For this, you need to have your eyes wide open. When your horse is new to you and you're completely infatuated, it can be difficult to see what's right in front of you with clarity. You may know this from your relationships with other people: it's easier to see clearly when you take off the rose-colored glasses. The moment those glasses come off isn't something to fear; that's when you and your horse can really start to get to know each other and start building a genuine relationship. Of course, this is only true if you're not just banking on quick success, but have a good inner attitude and plan on building a true, deep bond with your horse.

THE REALITY GUESSING GAME

Developing a horse correctly means structuring his behavior and giving him the security he needs to show us the behaviors we want and avoid the ones we don't. At its purest, it's simply about how we feel. A rearing horse might rear just because he's a horse. Maybe it gives him a special pleasure to rear, to feel his body and his strength. For a rider, however, a rearing horse can be very dangerous, and this can be a very scary behavior.

Let's say that rearing here stems from a functional pattern of pressure—then it might be a play behavior, or a test of strength. If we look at it as "wanting to get rid of the rider," then the same behavior may also be caused by defensiveness. These are all completely different root causes, but they have the same outcome. However, if the rider decides her horse reared because he was afraid, then she'll start to search for something that could have provoked his fear.

There's a lot of room here for misunderstandings. What if rearing stems from the functional pattern of aggressiveness or pushiness? In this case, you'd see a moving ear, a relaxed eye, blinking, strong yet relaxed muscle tension, and a relaxed tail without any indication of fear. (In the rider, on the other hand, we would probably see no blinking, intermittent breath holding, a rapid pulse, tight surface tension, and a high muscle tone.)

On the other hand, if the horse rears as a defensive gesture, then you'd see an overall tension in him as high as that of the rider I just described. He won't blink, his brow will be furrowed, he'll hold his breath, his tail will be swishing, and his mouth and nostrils will be tight. Of course, it's difficult to study your horse's eyelids while you're trying to sit on him—especially if he's rearing—but I still want to encourage you to observe his behavior as best you can, because this will determine whether you handle it correctly. If your horse rears because it's fun for him, he'll need clearer boundaries and possibly a more rigorous exercise regimen.

You can offer him both these things with in-hand work and with work on the

Say what you see to find your mistakes.

longe line. However, if your horse rears out of defensiveness, you need to try to figure out why he feels he has to defend himself. In this case, every detail, every training step, and every piece of equipment should be examined to look for a cause.

It's like writing a book: look at your work from as many angles as possible. Luckily, my family is very patient, and doesn't run away when I ask, "Can I read something to you?" Although I find their feedback very helpful, it's more than that. By reading out loud, I find errors and potentially confusing writing. When it comes to reading your horse, you can do it the same way. "Read"—or say what you're seeing—out loud, and listen to yourself. This is an astonishingly simple trick, and it may help you notice something you'd otherwise overlook.

THE RIDER'S FEAR

Usually in these situations, it's the rider who brings emotion into the conversation. It's understandable that most riders are frightened by a horse suddenly rearing, but don't forget that fear is actually a barrier to objectivity. It can alter our point of view and lead us into a tangle of misunderstandings, which it can be hard for us to see our way out of. While fear is a useful and necessary warning signal for us, too much fear can make us unpredictable to—and even aggressive toward—our horses.

Listen to Your Gut

Your gut is a great guide: when you feel fear start there, you should listen to it. It's part of our threat assessment system, and it can save your life. By contrast, fear that originates in the brain can sometimes be caused by a reminder of a previous experience. This kind of fear may not signal real danger, and can get in the way of the right thoughts and actions. It also deprives us of the ability to be objective. If you've ever sat on a horse that has reared defensively (which can be very scary!), then it will be extra hard for you to assess whether a horse is simply in a playful mood, testing, or showing his own strength by rearing. Your brain perceives the situation as dangerous, and you'll have a tough time thinking past that.

We can resolve this unwanted behavior only if we're able to objectively assess and respect the horse in question, and we can only do that if we can control our feelings and avoid projecting them onto the horse.

As information travels from the eye to the gut, a lot can go wrong—especially as it goes through the brain.

A loss of objectivity, combined with a horse that disrespects your aids, can quickly lead to fear, making a bad situation worse.

THE ROOT OF THE BEHAVIOR

Every expressive behavior can have different roots—which is to say, it can be prompted by different functional patterns. For example, the reason for a horse's rearing might be a pinching saddle, but the root of that behavior is a defensive functional pattern. Behavior needs to be closely examined to find this root cause; that's the only way to correct the horse's inner attitude. After we fix his pinching saddle, we're still stuck with the root of the behavior: that functional pattern that's been established. The horse has learned that rearing is a possible solution, and in the worst-case scenario, it may have become routine behavior. This is what needs to be thoroughly addressed.

THE TIP OF THE ICEBERG

This issue of root causes is why it's so important to fully understand all six functional patterns. That gives us objective knowledge of a horse's character. My system works best when you can find the right tools to create the work of art you hope to create. If our focus is on correcting inappropriate behavior, then we need to be able to differentiate between various possible root causes. If there is an issue with the horse's temperament, our job will be to thoroughly rebuild the horse's learning patterns.

For you as a trainer, this means checking for comparable behaviors in any other situation and correcting it every time, so the functional pattern the behavior stems from can no longer be considered a strategy for success by the horse. If you have a horse that uses rearing as a defensive strategy, then it makes sense to methodically check whether your horse has developed other defensive strategies. Most of the time, you will be able to find something, whether it's swishing his tail during saddling, squeezing his mouth shut during bridling, not wanting to lift his feet, or tension in the walk. With training in harmony, you'll address every symptom instead of only fixing the most distracting—but still superficial—problem. This way, you can find what lies beneath the tip of the iceberg, and correct the underlying issue.

"Grass doesn't grow faster if you pull on it."
—Ghanaian proverb

STRATEGIES FOR SUCCESS

We've talked about how horses think, and you've learned how many small steps it can take to get their happy cooperation. Think back to Hermann and Charlotte (page 100), or the beautiful liver chestnut mare Violetta (page 11) who refused to be bridled. These are classic examples of expectant defensive behavior. In Violetta's case, this behavior continued throughout her training. Not only did she not want to accept the bridle because of the pinching buckle, she also responded with hectic defensive behavior and used the same functional pattern when asked to accept contact, or when a leg aid was used. She would counter with a violent tail swish, she'd try to kick the rider's leg, or she would threaten to rear or buck. She was so defensive that she tried to thwart any attempt to interact with her.

FINDING THE CORRECT SOLUTION

Defensive behavior was her first reaction. It was her survival strategy. Maybe you've experienced this before, and had a horse that just wants to keep everyone away. This mare had had great success with her hectic and somewhat hysterical behavior. If the rider shortened the reins, she would throw up her head. If the rider added leg, she threatened to explode. Her rider reacted by giving her the reins and taking the leg off—in other words, Violetta's strategy was successful, and she got what she wanted. Because her rider became intimidated, this situation grew into a severe misunderstanding. From Violetta's perspective, defensive behavior was the correct answer, because humans stopped asking her questions every time she responded with this behavior. She must have been convinced her behavior was exactly what her human was looking for. Imagine the functional patterns like six exits off a roundabout: with Violetta, the exit labeled "Defensiveness" was well-traveled and two lanes wide, and the rest were one lane with no signs.

Because we were familiar with Violetta's reaction to bridling, we refused to let go of the reins, kept the leg aid quietly on, and just tolerated her threatening behavior without tension or anger. We met her with kindness, and showed her that her behavior was no longer a strategy for success. The moment she calmed down, we gave her a long rein, took leg off, and gave her lots of praise. It took a few lessons before the mare changed her approach; but she started to realize that there were multiple exits from the metaphorical roundabout that might be worthwhile, and she increasingly chose others instead.

Belvida's tension and defensiveness...

When we started to introduce flying changes a year and a half later, she experienced a setback; her defensive patterns resurfaced. She seemed overwhelmed, and her expectant defensive behavior once again stopped her from seeing the solution. She would get tight in the poll, run, and "steal" the change as soon as we tried to prepare for it. She stopped listening and became argumentative—we could tell she was anticipating the flying change exercises.

It put my patience to the test to have to come to a full halt every time she became frantic, but this is how we calmly showed her that her behavior wasn't the right answer. After that, every time she expected a flying change, we asked for something different: walk, volte, rein back, canter on. If she remained calm, then we would ask for a flying change, followed by a walk transition, a volte, a break, and praise. A few weeks like this felt like an eternity, but we kept at it, knowing it would pay off in the end.

EVERY STEP IS WORTHWHILE

This thorough, criticism-free approach is worth the time—every time, with every horse. Violetta repaid the patience we showed her with genuine devotion, an incredible willingness to perform, and unwavering loyalty.

Along the way, there were other misunderstandings that went much deeper and had negatively impacted her inner attitude. It was never just about acceptance of the aids, but about rebuilding her learning pattern with strategies that were productive for her training, not just successful for her. Defensive strategies can manifest several different ways. It's crucial to take the time to carefully address each strategy, thoroughly and empathetically. The six functional patterns are the basis for the horse's learning patterns. Even if I'm working with a horse who isn't a perfect model of success, I can help him develop better learning strategies.

As a trainer, I shouldn't be emotionally influenced by behavior, but I should be interested in that behavior and motivated to take a closer look, work even more carefully, and become even more objective. Leave the emotions to your horse. Make sure even misbehavior doesn't affect your attitude, so you can address the root of the problem. In this way, you can skillfully lead the dialogue with your horse, avoid misunderstandings, and create lasting and deep trust.

Here, you need skill and patience to produce positive energy.

Violetta is now a horse that can give confidence to others—what a huge success.

POSITIVITY PREVENTS MISUNDERSTANDINGS

It's important to avoid mistakes. It's also important to address them when they can't be avoided. Since we're not learning to ride a bike or cut wood, but rather to train living, independent creatures with their own ideas, and since we want to build happiness, every situation should be treated as fluid, and our job is ever-changing. It's important to accept that mistakes will happen.

Everyone is a product of the mistakes they've encountered in their lives—whether they were experiencing them or making them. Making mistakes is a natural part of learning. Let's call it trying something out, exploring boundaries, testing your own abilities, or testing systems. All of this is part of what creates our unique personalities. People make mistakes, and horses make mistakes.

You can tell how good a trainer is by how well he handles mistakes.

One thing is certain: Horses don't make mistakes to annoy people. They only make choices based on the options they perceive as available to them.

AVOIDING MISTAKES

You will fill many different roles for your horse. You might meet him on a social level as a friend or partner; then you may be a guardian; and the next moment, you're also a teacher. But what you should never be is his judge: you shouldn't be mentally scoring your horse. Dealing with misconduct requires a willingness to provide guidance, not grades. It's your training strategy—your overall approach—that determines whether you'll allow mistakes or avoid them in the first place. Both are effective methods.

THINKING POSITIVE

People who come to me for coaching usually describe their horse in negative terms: what hasn't been going well, or what's been hard. Successes are forgotten, dismissed, or maybe taken for granted, but they often don't get any attention in this initial report. If we imagine a scale with the positives on one side and the negatives on the other, it's usually tipped farther toward the negative side. This makes the rider focus on the negatives, essentially "pre-programming" her brain for failure.

☞ YOUR TRAINING DIARY

Remember to jot down positive situations in your training diary, regardless of how small and insignificant they may seem. Describe what went well in your sessions. Only after you do this should you think about what didn't go as well. Practice thinking progressive, dynamic, positive thoughts, which you can then follow up with positive behavior. Create a checklist that can help you avoid future mistakes.

Checklist 1: Avoiding Mistakes

— Overview of your space
— Age of the horse
— Level of horse's education
— Challenges
— Equipment
— External distracting factors
— Daily assessment of ability

Then, create a checklist for yourself.

Checklist 2: Self-Assessment

— How my space is organized
— Clarity of my use of three-dimensional language
— The four pillars and three elements of each
— Emotional objectivity
— Ability to read expressive behavior

With this protocol, you can coach yourself, and identify or avoid mistakes. Don't forget to view yourself in a positive light. Identify what you yourself do well and correctly, and what work you're happy with.

Provide guidance instead of criticism.

HANDLING MISTAKES

If you never make any mistakes, there's nothing to learn from. I want to motivate you to find positive solutions within the framework of the mistakes that are going to happen.

The best and simplest solution to help an animal that makes a mistake is to provide guidance. The most effective way to do this is through spatial orientation, because animals communicate primarily within this area. I can get a horse's attention by checking his responsiveness, direct his movement with spatial language, and signal relaxation with my body language. Getting the horse's attention and offering a spatial solution has the best results, in my experience, when it comes to creating calm and objectivity after a mistake.

RESPONSIVENESS WHEN UNDER "ATTACK"

Imagine you are sitting on your horse and suddenly someone opens an umbrella. The horse's head flies up and his neck gets tense, his ears are locked forward, and he

Positive experiences during competition can build cohesiveness and fuel teamwork.

turns toward this perceived danger. Your reaction should be to practice responsiveness by saying your horse's name and asking him to pay attention to you. If this works, praise him.

Responsiveness, attention-shifting, and rewardability are the correct tools for this situation. Should the horse not respond to his name, then you have discovered a problem.

It's in the nature of the horse to devote his full attention to the umbrella, and there's absolutely nothing wrong with that. Your horse should be able to process environmental stimuli. However, he should also learn to stay calm and on the aids despite distractions. This is where most people make mistakes, because in most cases, the horse's reaction to the umbrella's "attack" is punished, or else reinforced by the rider or handler attempting to calm the horse. Neither of these actions helps the horse manage the situation. Instead, redirect his attention. Say his name and expect him to promptly, happily, and correctly respond to you—don't forget these three elements of the response (page 40). If he doesn't answer appropriately, then you need to shift his attention to bring his focus to the sound of his name. This way, you enter a positive cycle, and you become the source of his happiness. Remember: always talk to him first, and shift his attention only if he doesn't react, before speaking to him again.

READ OUT LOUD

It can be helpful to describe your horse's expressive behavior to yourself out loud to find the cause of a mistake. This way, you put distance between your feelings and your observations. You'll notice in no time how easy it can be to develop a loving objectivity toward your horse. And remember the following saying: your best teacher is your most recent mistake.

LEARNING FROM EXPERIENCE

One year after Violetta moved in with us, her daughter Belvida arrived as well. The young mare made me think of Bambi: sweet, delicate, with huge round eyes. We prepared carefully before starting her under saddle. In-hand work and groundwork helped her connect with us and trust us. Everything was going so well; the work was simple and safe. Under saddle, Belvida worked with us like a ballerina—until, one day, a mistake snuck in somewhere.

Belvida developed massive tension when we tried to mount her from the ground, and she began bucking like a rodeo horse.

Be mindful of your horse. Always.

Carla had no chance to stay in the saddle. We were completely shocked. What had we missed, when we'd been working so carefully and thoroughly? Where was our mistake? We sorted ourselves out and started from scratch.

We worked one step at a time and read Belvida carefully. She stood quietly, and seemingly calmly, with relaxed ears and a soft eye. But as soon as Carla put one foot in the stirrup, Belvida stopped blinking. Her big, sweet Bambi eyes became huge and staring. Carla took her foot out of the stirrup, and Belvida started blinking again. Remember to also read what isn't there; until now, we had overlooked this tiny signal. We used a mounting block to repeat the exercise. Carla put one foot in the stirrup and waited until Belvida opened and closed those big doe eyes again. When Carla put weight in the stirrup and the mare stayed relaxed, Carla finished mounting. By using the mounting block and being gentle, we were able to continue Belvida's training.

Moving forward, there were no more incidents, and Belvida made no more mistakes. Or, rather, we never made this mistake again. We needed to pay more attention when mounting this particular horse, to give her a bit more time to give us her consent. We had become too confident in our routine because she had been so easy to work with, and we had stopped waiting for her. Whatever had bothered her, nothing would have happened had we slowed down a bit.

Recognizing every signal is crucial in training horses.

When we invest the time...

...our horses reward us by becoming reliable and safe.

Repetition is the mother of learning.

ONE STEP BACK, TWO STEPS FORWARD

In Belvida's case, we needed to make a spontaneous change to a specific situation. Since we recognized the mistake we had made early on in her training, and it had not yet been established as a habit, it was easy to fix. Finding a workable approach is usually easy; in this case, all we had to do was use a mounting block and wait for a moment after putting weight in the stirrup. Often, we must learn to take a step back. If mistakes crop up, it helps to read out loud and slowly take a step back, to better explain whatever topic we're training.

FIRST THE WHAT, THEN THE HOW

Divide learning into small steps; teach *what* first, and then *how*, and monitor your horse's learning curve. Stop the lesson while it's still going well to avoid fatigue for yourself and your horse. Never forget—you are your horse's coach, not his judge.

The way you handle mistakes will determine how well you progress with your horse. The same is also true of failure; take time to process and learn from whatever you failed at, so next time you can do better. Work more slowly, more thoroughly, and with greater empathy. Luckily, what happened with Belvida was easily resolved because we caught it early and we handled it thoughtfully. It's possible that something similar happened with Hermann (page 100). In his case, however, the mistake wasn't noticed in time to prevent it from developing into a fundamental problem with entrenched defensive behavior. How lucky for him that he eventually met Charlotte.

We are the masters of our own fate—our animals teach us this lesson daily. Good management and a good overall understanding of your horse's functional patterns are necessary for happy and harmonious training. The most important ingredient, however, is your positive attitude. This attitude will shape your actions, and will help you reach the goals you set for yourself and your horse.

Safety first—the only way to work with a young horse.

TOOLS FOR HAPPINESS

Look at the world from a different perspective—through the eyes of a horse. Notice the space, light, smells, and noises. Don't think of possible explanations based on what you know about these things; decouple your perceptions from your knowledge. For example, imagine a stormy day, and then picture hearing a very loud bang. A horse has no way of knowing that a storm is likely to bring lightning, and lightning means thunder. From his perspective, there's simply a sudden, loud noise that he may have never heard before, and he has no understanding of what it was or why it happened. His threat assessment system will be activated, and won't calm down again until he figures out he isn't in danger.

SAFETY THROUGH DIALOGUE

My system works through dialogue. What does that mean? We work on conscious access—a cognitive connection—to our horses. With well-developed responsiveness training, we will always be in a position to reach the horse on a cognitive level, to get him to concentrate and focus on us. With that alone are we able to give him safety.

Imagine a horse who has no such connection to his trainer, who has never learned to concentrate on or listen to anyone. He tries to flee when he gets frightened, but with a rider on his back, he realizes he can't get away. This alone can raise his stress level. Had this horse previously learned to concentrate on his human in moments of uncertainty, and to stay by his handler and seek out dialogue, then his nervous system would calm down very quickly.

From the point of view of the horse, some things humans don't even notice are potentially a threat. Since you have learned to notice the expressive behavior of your horse, it now becomes important to use the right tool at the right moment.

To keep the horse focused during exciting moments...

GUIDING THE HORSE DOWN THE PATH TO THE ANSWER

You notice tension developing, whether you're alongside or riding your horse. You see that he's looking at something—and I'll bet you look where your horse is looking, right? You want to know what's making him nervous. An old horseman once told me with a smile to stop doing this exact same thing, because, as he knew, this isn't the right way to guide a horse.

When your horse wants to pay attention to some external stimulus, say his name. Give him direction. In this moment, we usually see the one mistake the horse can make: he doesn't react to his name. This is when he needs his attention shifted, *not* reinforced (which is what happens when you look in the same direction he's looking); and even though he made a mistake, you must stay kind and calm. Shift his attention using your plan A and plan B (see page 36)—use a friendly, "With me," ask for space until he looks at you, and then give him back his space and invite him to come to you. You should always use this same procedure to guide the shift in the horse's attention.

PRACTICE: MASTERING DIFFICULT SITUATIONS AT HOME

When we practice potentially distracting situations in a controlled environment, we can be prepared and stay focused, and it's much easier for us to stay in dialogue with our horse. You can try, for example, asking someone to stand along the rail with an umbrella, opening it from time to time. Since you already know what's about to distract your horse, you can outsmart your own curiosity and practice keeping your focus completely on him.

Now practice the pillars you've already taught your horse: responsiveness, rewardability, attention-shifting, and attention to the aids. Don't look at the umbrella; instead, concentrate on your horse and on your dialogue with him, and give him spatial, cognitive, and emotional guidance. Allow your horse to look at the umbrella, say his name, and expect him to respond to you right away. Keep the three elements of his response in

...give space and work on rewardability...

...as your first and most important step.

mind. Be prepared to compromise a little bit on the third element, correct execution—but you want his answer to be immediate, and he should have the correct inner attitude.

LEADERSHIP AND WILLINGNESS TO COMPROMISE

A successful trainer needs to be able to lead and willing to compromise. Make requests of your horse that he can easily fulfill. Giving you his full attention with calm focus is an easy lesson, and you should insist on it, because these two things are the first two of the three elements you want in his response. Don't worry about whether his reaction leads to the exact behavior you're looking for, at least initially. We can work that out in the next "umbrella session." If he doesn't listen, remember plan A and plan B, and only then start to shift your horse's attention and request space. Give that space back to him only when he's paying attention again.

DIRECTION, SPACE, AND BOUNDARIES

Don't focus solely on your horse's direction or path in this situation. The most important means of communication for your horse is spatial communication. Tell him not to come into your space. Hold your space and ask for space to help him relax. You can compromise by giving him space, too. In this way, you offer your horse the positive, clear, species-appropriate boundaries that will calm his threat assessment system and activate his bonding system.

If your horse turns to look at the umbrella, he's taken charge by changing his direction and taking his focus off of you. If you want to explain to your horse that the umbrella is not a threat, then you should work on getting him to focus on you again and stay on the correct line of travel. Don't forget to stop when it's going well.

In plain language: If your horse does this well, then put the umbrella aside and do something your horse enjoys to finish out the session. If your horse doesn't manage this task well, then ask your helper to slowly increase the distance between the two of you and the umbrella bit by bit until you have the horse's focus. In this situation, you're making sure the umbrella is outside the horse's defensive zone so he will stop feeling like he has to react to it. Carefully figure out the size of this zone. Review the activation and defensive zones (page 61), and work in these areas calmly and without expectation. Let your horse know you are making sure he succeeds.

Work with your horse, not against him. When your horse relaxes, you've found the activation zone. Here, you can address his responsiveness and allow the umbrella to come closer step by step. This way, you sow seeds that will grow into trust.

Giving space also means the horse should...

...quickly close the gap.

Finding activation zones: an exercise that puts the horse on the right track with playful consistency.

PRACTICE: THE COMPASS TO HAPPINESS

I call this basic in-hand exercise "the compass." Stand in the center of the arena, regardless of the size of the space, with your horse by your side, either on the right or the left. Now, you work each of the points of a compass (north, east, south, west): make a quarter-turn on the spot in such a way that your horse can either give or take space. With every correctly executed quarter-turn, stop and praise your horse profusely. This exercise, which requires very little space, trains your spatial thinking, your understanding of your horse's path, and your horse's ability to stay in the desired space.

Once this is easy for you, you can start to add in more distractions, and explain to your horse that no matter what is happening around you, you are his safe place, because you oversee and control the space around him. This is a kind way to work with your horse: it gives him security and guidance, and uses a means of communication he understands to share information with him. It offers him a safe external environment and an engaged, positive internal environment.

THE TRAINING SCALE

Just as the classical training scale is used when we work with the horse under saddle, it can be used with training in-hand and groundwork. This scale is a common thread, a guide; it serves as a navigational aid on our journey. With this in mind, though, it's important to allow for some variation in each individual journey. The training scale has six components, with each building on the last; you'll see them given different names by different trainers, but in this book, I will call them:

— Rhythm
— Relaxation
— Connection
— Impulsion
— Straightness
— Collection

The training scale is the foundation of correct training and should be valued as such. However, it's primarily focused on the physical development of the horse's gaits. The only training stage in the list that also involves the horse's inner attitude is relaxation, because a horse can only be relaxed physically if he's relaxed mentally.

My system leans on these principles. The training scale is a proven, logical, and clear guide. The only thing it doesn't give you is a straightforward way to communicate with the horse's mind, which is what allows a trainer to work on relaxation in a way that works with and not against the horse's nature. The training scale is a wonderful tool, and I see no need to reinvent the wheel, but I find it useful to include a second scale in my system, dedicated to the correct development of the horse's inner attitude. This training scale for working with a horse on the ground is structured as follows:

— Willingness to communicate
— Organization of space
— Comfort zone behavior and bonding
— Inner attitude
— Staying on the path of travel
— Lessons based on the principle of making an offer

We can increase responsiveness...

...by working on attention-shifting, re-focusing...

...and rewardability, which creates a true bond.

Once you have tackled these topics, you can dedicate yourself to your individual training plan and build up your horse to best suit whatever his role will be. This is a training scale aimed at successful dialogue; if horse training is a dialogue, then we should develop the necessary vocabulary before any other training begins.

THE USE OF SPACE

The systematic training of a horse is a step-by-step exchange of information. We use clear, species-appropriate means of communication to convey information, and we read expressive behavior without judgment to receive information from the horse. Most people need help recognizing and correctly using space. This is where humans tend to have the biggest deficits.

The most common mistake is giving space. Often, we do this without intending to, in order to get a bit more distance from our horse. We don't even need to take a step to make this mistake; just moving one foot backward is enough. This immediately signals to the horse that you are defensive and not ready to hold your space, not ready to enforce boundaries, or even that you want to invite him into the space you're giving up. To use correct spatial communication, remember:

- Keeping space means holding your position.
- Demanding space means you want to step into the horse's footsteps.
- Giving space means making room, to step aside and to offer a spot in the newly available space.

By correctly using spatial communication, you can provide your horse with the rules and boundaries he needs.

With a healthy bond, we can calm the threat assessment system. A worthwhile lesson.

THE HORSE'S INNER ATTITUDE

Dialogue should always take precedence over anything else. A horse's best trick counts for nothing if his inner attitude is wrong. We see this training as the basis for preparing a horse for life; he should learn to be open to bonding, relaxed, and willing to perform, so he can be in a healthy and strong partnership with his trainer. Some people want to focus on sport and performance, while others want friendship and a deep emotional bond with their horse. The way I see it, both of these scenarios require that a horse be willing to bond, which he can only do if his bonding system is strong and healthy. Find out what type of relationship you are ready for. No matter what the answer is, you will need my training scale to create specific goals and chart a successful path forward.

☞ YOUR TRAINING DIARY

- Clearly define for yourself how you envision your relationship with your horse.
- Determine which points on the training scale work well already.
- Figure out where you still have gaps in your training.
- Look at the point prior to the one that needs work and evaluate it thoroughly.
- Monitor your communication within training. Define what you did well and search for any misunderstandings.
- Monitor your horse's performance curve, as well as your own as rider or handler. Check your own expressive behavior.

MOTIVATION: MAKING IT FUN

We have spoken a lot about the horse's inner attitude—both how to understand it and how to affect it—but now I want to focus on you. I want to devote myself to your way of thinking and the actions you take.

Nearly everyone who comes to me for coaching has a problem with a horse. In their descriptions, I hear complaints, frustrations, difficulties, and sometimes even blame. Sure, if you don't have any problems, you probably don't need help in the first place; but these early descriptions often reveal the dark side of the relationship. When I ask the question, "What do you like about your horse?" many people seem to wake up. They look at me, and then at the horse, and then at me again. It takes them some time to put it into words, and it's often quite subjective. But this is exactly the point: occasionally we need to put on those rose-colored glasses, enjoy the warm fuzzies, notice the successes, and feel the happiness our horses bring us. If you're going to do the work of establishing an emotional relationship, it's important to cultivate these feelings.

"There are many paths to happiness. One of them is to stop complaining."

—Unknown

Animals instinctively mirror positive energy.

If you're still reading this book, chances are you're hoping for more than a working relationship with your horse. You're probably hoping for something that resembles a partnership.

MAKING YOUR OWN LUCK

You can influence your own thoughts. You can structure and train your brain. Your mind filters what you perceive: if, for example, you're interested in a new car, then you'll see cars you are interested in everywhere. If you're hoping to have children, you'll suddenly see families with kids everywhere. If you're caring for an elderly person, then you'll start to notice everything that makes life harder or easier for an aging person. If you've experienced a loss, suddenly every program you watch seems to deal with the same kind of loss. Your brain filters for things that are relevant to your situation.

Use a positive outlook to help you master difficult lessons.

The same thing happens with success and failure, joy and sadness.

Along these lines, if you can work to develop positive thoughts, you'll start to notice significantly more positive things around you.

In turn, as you notice more positive things, your body will express more positive energy. Step up with a more positive attitude and you'll get back more positive reactions in return. It is as if you're creating your own good luck.

THE BRIGHT SIDE OF LIFE

Start training your own thoughts with simple exercises. List what's making you happy, what's good, and what feels harmonious. Write down something positive as soon as you get up each morning, for a week, a month, the next few years... Focus on the positive.

☞ YOUR TRAINING DIARY

Set up pages in your journal for positive moments: rephrase them and repeat them. Define your vision for your partnership with your horse through a positive lens, and make these positives the goal of every training session. Train your thoughts.

LOOKING IN THE MIRROR

Your horse, as a specialist in spatial and physical language, is always able to read your expressive behavior. Maybe he doesn't always tell you what he reads from you, but he adapts his behavior each time. He'll always reflect what you show him back to you. This "mirroring" provides you with prompt, honest feedback. Try to see this as an opportunity, because horses will always tell you how you come across.

Enthusiasm for the work you do creates a true partnership.

WHEN HORSES GIVE US COMPLIMENTS

If you approach a horse with positive energy, radiating confidence, equilibrium, and mindfulness, then your horse will reflect that energy back to you. Horses never seek contact with tension, stressors, or emotional burdens. A horse wants to maintain equilibrium between his inner and outer environments. If his person is radiating frustrations or resentment at him, then this balance is in trouble.

Take it as a compliment if your horse seeks you out and shows he enjoys being with you. Return the compliment sincerely and extensively, and above all, enjoy it, because it comes from a huge heart.

Confidence is like a muscle. It needs to be exercised daily.

The basics in every partnership—direction, space, and boundaries—should be checked frequently...

LEARNING FROM EXPERIENCE

Suzanne has been working with me with both her dogs and her horses for over ten years. When I first met her, she stood out as one of the rare people who never complained about their animals. She came to me that first time with her Fjord, Flocke. During that first session, when I asked her what she wanted to achieve, she replied, "Everything!" She laughed as she tried to calm her horse. The little mare, however, preferred to step on Suzanne's toes, push into her, and pull away from her. She told me the horse had been a wedding gift, and she thought the mare was just amazing. She was totally in love with Flocke's strong personality, but she had a lot to learn.

Flocke Gives Us a Warning

As soon as Flocke could, she tore herself free and ran into the nearest corner. Once there, she aimed her croup in Suzanne's direction. It was fairly easy to hear what she was telling us: "Stay away." It took a lot of persuasion to get her out of that position. She had a short, tight, strong neck, on top of which she carried a head full of her own stubborn ideas.

Flocke already knew Suzanne couldn't match her physical strength. Because of that, the external environment wasn't a safe one, and Suzanne was unable to establish boundaries. If Flocke decided to leave, she simply straightened herself, pushed Suzanne away with her inner shoulder, and ran off. What was truly wonderful was that Suzanne wasn't frustrated by this. She sought out solutions so she could do better. First solution: we switched out her lead for one that had a chain we could run under Flocke's chin.

This way, Suzanne had a better chance when Flocke tried to overpower her.

...with a friendly giving and taking of space.

Connecting and Controlling the Conversation

Suzanne didn't use the chain to pull Flocke toward her, but rather to shut the "outside" doors. As soon as Flocke was focused more "inward," Suzanne lavished her with praise. It was these first steps that made dialogue between them possible. After a few sessions, Flocke basically abandoned her attempts to push Suzanne away. Suzanne learned to recognize Flocke's intention to move earlier, and opened the door to the "inside" by giving a little space and by stopping or turning. By turning, she explained to Flocke that she was quite capable of closing doors, and controlling the use of space and tempo.

Direction, Space, and Rules

I am convinced it was Suzanne's blame-free approach and her positive, playful attitude toward Flocke that brought Flocke back to the conversation again and again. First things first: we had to work on Flocke's attentiveness, so that every time we lost her, we could get her attention back. Then we started to work on leading. From the left, it was easy, but from the right, the mare reverted to her old pushy behavior. However, unlike in that first lesson, Suzanne now knew how to counter Flocke's ideas about moving away before they became a problem. Flocke quickly came to realize right and left worked the same way, and walking off wasn't a correct answer from either side. She learned to maintain her space next to Suzanne, accepted Suzanne's direction and path of travel, and saw her human more and more as a leader.

Fitness for Flocke

This horse was also desperately out of shape and needed to build muscle and strength. And so the cycle always goes, with any horse: we school the inner bond, establish a comfort zone, create a training path, and then begin to build fitness, because we want to create true athletic partners. This lovely Norwegian girl developed beautifully through cavaletti training, communicative longeing, and trail riding. Good training kept unlocking better results.

The more Flocke stayed with her, the better Suzanne was able to work with her.

To do what you like is freedom.
To like what you do is happiness.

Teaching difficult lessons using playful consistency creates an opportunity for deep bonding.

The more engaging the task, the more willing Flocke was to focus on Suzanne. Work in-hand and groundwork progressed quickly. The bow was easy to explain, but when we tried to teach her to lie down, we met our favorite old functional pattern again: aversive pushiness (bossy behavior to avoid the task).

FLOCKE AND SUZANNE

Team:
Flocke, 12-year-old Fjord mare
Suzanne, ambitious amateur equestrian

Communication issues:
- Pushiness and lack of boundaries
- Defensive, passive threats
- Expressive behavior
- Tight body, not listening

Training path:
- Learn to read expressive behavior of the horse and react appropriately
- School rewardability, work on bonding
- Work on creating predictability and boundaries, define and hold one's space, maintain the path
- Work on the ground, at liberty, and add strength training

Suzanne asked Flocke to bow, and then asked if she could bend her second knee as well and kneel completely. Flocke's response was a resounding "no." She stood up quickly and escaped into a corner. Suzanne didn't immediately follow her the way she used to do. Instead, she slowly tested the boundaries of Flocke's activation zone—the distance that provoked a slight response from Flocke. (She was careful to avoid Flocke's defensive zone.) She then turned her own body in the desired direction and said, "Walk on." Flocke looked at her and proceeded to walk in the desired direction. Suzanne walked alongside her on the inside of the arena and gradually—with very small steps—moved closer to her. When she was finally able to get close without Flocke speeding up, she asked her to halt: "And halt." Flocke stopped moving, because she had learned this signal when learning to lead. When Flocke halted, Suzanne approached her and gave her tons of praise.

Convincing the Horse

It was a failure that Flocke had pushed open the closed door and refused to kneel, but it was a huge success that this previously habitual conflict could be resolved with a peaceful and even loving dialogue.

This moment was, although somewhat accidental, her first foray into liberty work. She used three-dimensional language and was clear and non-threatening. She showed Flocke the space and the path they should take as a team. It was a real "a-ha!" moment for both of them.

The next time I asked Flocke to lie down, I added a longe line to make sure both human and horse stayed in the classroom. Flocke tried two or three more times to resist by pushing away, but when she found the actual solution, she simply lay down for us.

During these months working together, Suzanne had always been happy and smiling, but in that moment, when her mare lay down for her, it was as if the sun grew even brighter. This little moment was so powerful. Only horse people understand how big these small moments truly are.

Building Trust from Scratch

It was Suzanne's attitude toward Flocke that made training seem almost effortless. Her contagious *joie de vivre* allowed so much positive energy to be part of even very difficult moments, and her lack of rigid goals allowed her to introduce a great deal of variety into her training. Yes, she had to explain the concept of space to her naughty mare, regulate distances, and train her to listen. But she successfully explained every step of my training scale to Flocke, and she learned to play with her. She eventually earned enough trust from this little Fjord that in addition to teaching her to lie down, she was able to teach Flocke to piaffe, to lie flat on her side, to work at liberty, and to follow alongside while her handler rode a bike.

The path is always the same—except Suzanne made her path safe and interesting in the truest senses of the words.

BE A SAFE PLACE

Imagine the feeling of having a really comfortable home: a place where you can be your true self and be loved, respected, and understood as you are; a cozy place that feels like entering a warm kitchen where there's always a cup of cocoa ready to be poured and something delicious baking in the oven. Be such a place for your horse, blame-free and loving, always ready to provide safety and comfort. Train your thoughts to focus on the positive aspects of your horse that you want to nurture and develop; take these thoughts with you as your horse's world expands beyond the stable walls.

☞ YOUR TRAINING DIARY

To motivate yourself and your horse:

- List seven positive things—every day—from your work with your horse.
- Choose one problem or difficulty, and search for the cause.
- Address one problem at a time.
- Think about what you did well yourself.
- Remember the moments that felt good and worked well for you, and make a note of them as a reminder of success.

Attaining the true goal: a trusting relationship.

Three different species, one happy bond.

WORKING AT LIBERTY

It was time for Suzanne and Flocke to begin liberty work. Liberty dressage is where training in harmony can be elevated to an art form. What is it that makes working at liberty so special? Is it the revelation of the real dialogue between horse and human, the focused communication; the respectful, informal togetherness that comes together like a beautiful dance, full of energy and elegance? Or is it the invisible bond that brings two beings together? Perhaps it's because this is where you can truly see genuine affection between two very different species.

> *"Ask me to show you poetry in motion, and I will show you a horse."*
>
> *—Unknown*

WHEN TRAINING BECOMES ART

To ride a horse with the subtlest aids, to channel his energy, to feel the dynamic power of his gaits—to a horseperson, this feels like true happiness. But if we then take off his tack and call him, and he comes eagerly to us, it's so much more than happiness. It's truly humbling; it's love.

But what exactly is work at liberty? It's the ability to focus the mind of another creature. It's being able to direct and influence the horse's movement. Liberty work is the result of successfully trained responsiveness and well-trained spatial language. As with all art, when it's done well, it looks easy—you can't tell how much effort it took. However, work at liberty doesn't have to be that difficult if you're careful and systematic. It's in a horse's nature to focus on a leader—to join up—as we learned in the chapter on bonding. So, once again, we make use of the laws of a horse's natural language.

The path to freedom doesn't start with freedom. Let's take a look at how we got from there to here: what do you need to start working at liberty? At first: a secure spot, a safe fence, a halter, a lead rope, and a whip. After you've established the basics of the four pillars (page 30) as well as leading, address the use of space: holding space, asking for space, and giving space.

Then you can move on to turning. Turning is the key to freedom, because with this, you'll be able to shut the "outside" door for the horse every time he might have gone there.

DEFINING SPACE

Imagine there are rooms to the right and left of you, and one in front of you (which I call home, because this is the room where we provide comfort zone training). If you lead your horse, he should walk to either the right or the left of you. As our mare Daily

Spatial organization and...

...communication form the foundation for work at liberty.

(page 54) explained to us quite well, horses instinctively understand this positioning. A position by your side gives your horse a feeling of safety, and your direction describes his trajectory.

Just remember this simple formula: first direction, then space, and finally radius.

This means you will learn to think about direction (clockwise and counterclockwise), relative position (right and left), and distance (how close the horse is to you). During liberty work, you use all three. Let's start with a lesson the horse has already learned: walk toward the point of his shoulder, saying, "Walk on," to ask him to give you space. This easy lesson checks an important pillar on which his entire education is built—establishing boundaries.

LEADING

Remember to always position yourself at your horse's shoulder to lead him; from this vantage point you can:

— read your horse
— reach the front and back of your horse
— drive him forward

This position is highly effective for commanding space and tempo. While quietly and gently leading your horse, school the signals to walk on, halt, and turn. The acoustic signals while leading could be, for example, "Walk on," "And halt," and "And turn" (see the vocabulary list on page 68).

TURNING

Stand by your horse's shoulder, on his left side, with the whip in your left hand and the lead in your right. Turn toward your horse without leaving your space. As you turn, "close the door" in front of the horse with the whip and say, "And turn." You should turn without stepping forward or back, which conveys that you're holding your space: you are turning clockwise on your own axis. Your horse should turn around you so you end up on his right side.

While your horse is turning, carefully exchange the lead and the whip so the whip ends up in front of your horse again. If you want your horse to turn from right to left, you will rotate counterclockwise around your own axis. You may want to practice this exercise with another person first so you're comfortable with each step and you're sure the spatial language will be unambiguous to the horse.

GIVING SPACE AND CREATING A PULL TO THE INSIDE

Now move away from your horse and ask him to follow you. Essentially, you are giving him space, as if inviting him to join you on your personal island. You want your horse to understand what you're saying to him: "I can close certain doors and send you in another direction. By choosing to go that direction, you can make me—and therefore yourself—happy." This should be a game of push and pull. Although you're putting yourself in a position of dominance, don't turn the horse to ask for space, because that won't create a pull to the inside—that is, that won't draw him toward you. When you turn your horse, you're inviting him to come toward you. Take advantage of a horse's natural tendency to come to the inside to get your horse interested in this new game.

COMMUNICATIVE LONGEING

We build on the skill of turning while leading when we teach communicative longeing. It's the exact same process, except that we replace the lead rope with a longe line. Practice this first calmly at the walk, in a ring or field with good walls or fencing. Keep your horse on a small circle until he can reliably change direction when you ask. I explain leading, traditional longeing, and communicative longeing in detail in my book *Wenn Pferde Komplimente machen* [When Horses Bow to You].

USING COMMUNICATION PATHWAYS

Let's revisit the three communication pathways: to ask your horse to turn, first give the horse a spatial signal (close the door with the whip), then a physical one (turning your body's axis in the new direction of movement), and finally an acoustic one ("And turn"). In order to successfully work at liberty—the ultimate goal—you'll need clear acoustic signals.

For longeing, change the order in which you use these signals: First, give the acoustic signal ("And turn"), and only then hold the whip in front of your horse. Finally, turn your body's axis in the new direction, looking where the horse should go. To summarize, for longeing: acoustic first, then body language, and finally spatial.

GOOD LISTENING

This work will accomplish something crucial: your horse will learn to listen very well. Every time you notice your horse is oriented toward the "outside," turn his attention back toward you—the inside.

In communicative longeing, I work on attentiveness...

... and create an inward pull by turning the horse toward me...

...so the horse comes to understand that "inward" is the solution.

If I open the door that leads toward me with my body language, then the horse should follow this pull to the inside.

This will school your spatial thinking as well as the responsiveness of your horse. Your horse will realize that you can close the path to the "outside" and you will always provide him with an "inside." This has a big effect on his willingness to be guided by you. He'll learn you can calculate spatially just as well as another horse, and you're in control of your space and your timing. All this aside, he'll also appreciate your taking charge; he'll think you are a safe place to be because you always return the space you take, creating comfort zones for him to operate in.

MAKING REQUESTS

When we make a request, we use two pillars of basic training: responsiveness and rewardability. The horse's name is what we might call a "pulling aid," and it's one he learned at the beginning of his education, when we first addressed responsiveness (page 31). If you want your horse to come to you, call him by his name and walk backward.

With the whip, just like when you were turning on a circle, you close off the direction of travel on the circle so that, geometrically, you create a triangle. This works similarly to the ground crew helping park an airplane: you free up the space you want your horse to enter, and use the "pull" created by turning and following inward. The horse is familiar with this from your earlier work on turning, and he will turn toward you. Because you're giving space, he'll move toward you—he'll follow you. Once he has reached you, let him come "home" (into the space in front of you), giving him a large dose of comfort. Then position yourself at his shoulder (the space where you eventually want him to "park"), and proceed with rewardability.

So far, you've used three pillars of my training system: responsiveness, rewardability, and establishing boundaries (accepting the aids). Only the fourth one remains. In a playful way, your horse learns to move toward the spaces you give him. Everything is still safe; you're in a quiet setting, and your relaxed, attentive horse is wearing a halter and secured with the longe line.

SIGNALING A TURN

Once the horse truly understands and has internalized responsiveness and rewardability, and is open to bonding, I teach him to respond to a request for a U-turn, and I train this as part of bonding. After a thorough warm-up, I bring the horse into the middle of the arena and take a moment to practice rewardability by scratching his dock (the bony part of his tail). To both sides of the base of the tail, the horse has a large number of oxytocin-producing glands. Scratching this area releases these hormones, making it a great way to work on rewardability with your horse. Maybe you've noticed your horse standing head to tail next to his buddy, each grooming the other around their tail area. This is a nice bonding ritual between good friends, and we can copy it. After riding, I'll ask my horse if I can scratch his dock. If he lifts his tail, then he's telling me he's very relaxed, and I happily accept the compliment and look forward to our next session. If he doesn't, then I reflect on my training and try to do better next time.

Now for the request. Our work on bonding and this comfort zone ritual are preparation for making a request. I position myself behind my horse and activate the dock as described above. The moment he lifts his tail, I stop, because we live by the slogan, "Stop when it's going well." Now I step three feet back, giving him space, and I turn my upper body so I'm offering my shoulder to him, showing him the space he should enter as I call his name. I'll still use the halter and lead rope to keep him from walking in a different direction than the one leading directly to me. Because our bonding efforts have worked well so far, I'm sure my horse will turn around and come to me in response to me giving him space and calling his name. Once he arrives, he gets immediately rewarded.

THE ATTENTIVE HORSE

All of these steps—the turning toward, the attentiveness, the pull to the inside, and the open connection—are fundamentally important elements of my system, and are therefore crucial for liberty work as well. Attentiveness is a learning process. It can be the result of a natural bond, like the kind you see in life-long couples who have spent years together, but it

Successful bonding with your horse means he'll see you as his refuge.

☞ THE GEOMETRY OF LANGUAGE

Clearly expressing ourselves with our bodies—correctly recognizing and regulating spaces with physical language—ensures our horses can easily understand us. The following examples show the different positions we can take when leading. These first steps lay the foundation for work at liberty.

A soft, relaxed body that holds space at the horse's shoulder. From this position, the handler can access physical reward points on the neck, shoulder, and withers.

Space is given by turning on our axis in the direction we would like to send the horse. A voice command can support this.

In the driving position, the handler's axis is turned in the desired direction of movement, while she moves toward the horse's ribs.

When asking for a turn, the handler's outside shoulder directs the movement of the horse, and her axis turns in the desired direction.

When asking for space, the handler's outside shoulder blocks the horse's current path and her positioning on her axis requests space from the horse.

When holding space, the handler's body calmly and clearly indicates both direction and space, which provides security for the horse.

When asking for a turn in the opposite direction, it's the same process both physically and spatially, performed counter-clockwise instead (or vice versa).

When inviting, the handler turns her body and gives space, offering the horse her shoulder as a "landing place." Once the horse comes into this space, the handler gives him plenty of praise.

can also happen thanks to intensive bonding work and successful training. Good communication is based on the principle of attentiveness. Remember, as someone who hopes to build harmony and happiness through your training, your tools (responsiveness and rewardability) are crucial to creating true dialogue by teaching attentiveness.

ATTENTION-SHIFTING

If your horse pushes outward, calmly and kindly use an acoustic signal to shift his attention, such as "Hey, hey," then close the door to his outside with the lead rope and the door in front of him with the whip. It's important for you to maintain your space, not threaten your horse, and give him the time he needs to choose his new path. Then use the signal, "And turn," to help your horse find the answer to your question. This way, your horse learns to let his attention be shifted by your signal and to turn toward you. The attention-shifting signal will be worth its weight in gold later, when you want to re-direct your horse after he makes a mistake. Even though he knows how to turn at this point, this exercise explains your attention-shifting signal to your horse in a new way, with a new vocabulary.

THE TRAFFIC LIGHT AGAIN

Let's revisit my traffic light method (page 36) and repeat the process briefly to clarify your use of language; it's important to differentiate between your attention-shifting signals.

1. "With me"—which we learned to use while leading—prepares the horse to be touched with the whip. It's the yellow phase of the traffic light, when you are using driving aids.
2. "Hey, hey," is also the yellow phase, but is intended to draw the horse's attention to the fact that I am about to close the door in front of him. I use this signal when I want to turn a horse that is trying to push out.

DIRECTION AND SPACE

Once I have schooled the lessons described above, I can start introducing basic liberty work with the horse by leading him without a lead rope, walking next to his shoulder, inside a 15 x 15-meter round pen or paddock. Using three-dimensional signals—the

To share your thoughts with your horse about the space you're using...

...is spatial communication.

acoustic signal, "Walk on," the body language signal of my body axis facing ahead, and the spatial signal of holding my space next to him—I can show him the direction I want him to go, and we'll begin to walk.

I need to make sure I keep him in front of my driving aids. Then I show him where he should be through my use of space. I can tell him whether I want him to the right or left of me, and whether I want to turn him or move him away from the wall. I incorporate more and more turning so I can influence his outside. I can close the "outside" door, because my horse has learned to choose a new path toward me instead of pushing away.

CHANGING ONE VARIABLE AT A TIME

This lesson usually goes fairly well, fairly quickly—and that may make you stumble into a common trap: you may feel like the master of liberty work and get a little overconfident. This is when it can be easy to make big mistakes. It can be tempting to ask too much too quickly, taking away the time the horse needs to decide on his new path inward. That is when he might choose the wrong path, the outward path, instead. Working at liberty requires a slow, steady, systematic approach. Further development should be done in small steps. There are a few different variables that can be changed, but you should change them one at a time. For example, if I want to change the setting, the distance, or the number of distractions around us, I'll pick just one and add the lead rope back into the equation again.

THE LITTLE BONDING GAME

We use a foolproof, uncomplicated game with our horses every day; we call it "The Little Bonding Game." Anyone can play it,

Through the combination of targeted rewardability...

...and giving space so he freely follows...

...the path toward me will become the horse's own idea.

Bonding is like a muscle—
it needs to be exercised to grow strong.

anytime and anywhere, and it always does the trick. Start by standing next to your horse and scratching him. Praise him until the praise takes effect and your horse's expressive behavior clearly shows relaxation. Then stop abruptly and walk a foot or two off to the side, still facing him.

Your horse will follow you and ask you to continue scratching him, and you'll happily oblige. Once again, scratch him in a favorite spot until his expressive behavior shows relaxation, at which point you'll give him some more space. This game is limitless. As your horse's behavior becomes more reliable, you can start to change the angle and distance that you move, so your horse has to work a little harder each time to get his reward from you.

Incorporate this little bonding game into your liberty work as often as possible. It's like interval training in horseback riding, where we use breaks to ensure deep well-being and relaxation. And remember, this isn't just time spent snuggling with your horse, it's bonding work.

Bonding work is the most profitable investment you can make in your partnership.

FREE LONGEING

Once the horse understands use of space, leading, and turning at liberty in my 15 x 15-meter pen, I'll start working circles at liberty. As before with communicative longeing, I let my horse walk around me in a circle. My body's axis points in the direction I want him to move. Again, I indicate which direction I want him to go first; then I give space, followed finally by a change in the radius, meaning a little more distance from me. The acoustic signal is, "Walk on," the body language is a driving gesture, and the spatial signal is to hold or minimally request space—but this time, point at the horse's hip instead of at his elbow. I work within the horse's activation zone, and gently maintain this pressure.

The horse should already be familiar with this expressive behavior from communicative longeing. If I want to turn my horse, I move in front of him, turn my body's axis in the direction I want him to go, and tell him, "And turn." Pay careful attention to the distance between you. Don't get too close to him, and choose your distance in such a way that he will find it easy to turn toward the inside.

Now I study my horse's expressive behavior, because I want to understand what his intention is when it comes to movement. I keep my horse on the circle until I notice him putting more weight on his outside limbs, meaning he wants to move out more. This is when I'll ask him to turn, and after each of these turns, I either give him space or play the bonding game with him. You'll find it can be easy to convince a horse it's fun to bond—to be affectionate and responsive. The most important factor, however, is still the safe outside, as well as solid inner bond. As our confidence together increases, I gradually add more variables—for example, walk to trot, and once that goes well, the canter. The signal words for these gaits were taught during his early education, so we can now use them during work at liberty.

I concentrate on the horse's focus and call on him regularly, to not only teach him to focus on me, but also praise him and bring harmony into our work together.

By finding comfort inside and having a safe outside, the horse learns to travel on a circle at liberty.

While doing so, he follows the spatial instructions I give him with my body language.

DIALOGUE AND FREEDOM

Once we understand work at liberty as a respectful dialogue, it becomes a harmonious partnership. When it's genuine *liberty* work, you'll see the beauty and majesty of a horse who is making his own choices—who is free, not held by invisible chains.

Work at liberty offers us a system in which we can show the horse spaces and paths he can evaluate and choose for himself. He learns to make his trainer the center of his thinking as he assesses these possibilities. His center is his home: his safe and pleasant inside. As his center, we can demarcate outside boundaries for him through good spatial thinking and sophisticated spatial language. This is where the beauty of liberty work becomes unmistakable and easy to see.

Give a safe framework for freedom and the freedom for a safe framework.

I want to be their favorite person—a friend to them.

THE FOUNDATIONS OF LIBERTY WORK

- Learn what your horse's spatial expressiveness looks like at liberty in order to catch any attempt to turn away from you early on and redirect it so he learns to turn toward you.
- Work the space: hold, give, and ask for space.
- Be careful to consistently use clear and correct language; reduce acoustic signals as you systematically apply three-dimensional language.
- Practice and monitor the four pillars and the three elements of each; they're the fundamentals of your training.
- Create a safe and comfortable inside and safely and proactively limit the outside.
- Practice intensive bonding work and comfort zone training.
- Change only one variable at a time, and stay in a safe setting for as long as needed.
- Work in short, clear intervals. Monitor your horse's performance curve. Stop when it's going well.
- Read your horse's expressive behavior. Respond positively to every gesture of affection and every active offer.

When you seek closeness, move away from the horse a little bit and invite him to come to you. Create a positive pull toward you, the inside. If you seek distance from your horse, move toward him and ask quietly and kindly for space. Avoid the temptation to approach him to seek closeness, or move away to create distance.

Remember: Liberty work isn't about creating a submissive horse, but rather a self-confident partner who is open to holding a spatial, physical, and acoustic dialogue with you. The horse should become a happy, beautiful creature to behold as a result of your training.

WHAT DO I DO WHEN…

- my horse won't turn toward me?
- my horse keeps running away?
- my horse won't relax when I praise him?
- my horse evades me?
- my horse constantly moves into my path?
- my horse won't accept my driving aids?
- my horse won't react to his name?

There's an easy answer to all these questions: make the space where you work smaller, keep the halter and lead rope on, and go back to the basics. Take your time and figure out exactly where a mistake was made.

Have you explained the space properly? Did you remove the halter or lead rope too soon? Have you paid close attention to your own path and trajectory? Have you noticed and corrected your horse's deviations from his path quickly enough? Have you trained the driving aids properly, according to my traffic light system (page 32), so an acoustic signal is enough? Have you identified (and do you respect) your horse's activation and defensive zones? Have you created a pull to the inside, and have you shown your horse the path to home, to you?

THE MAGIC OF LIBERTY

I have often wondered what exactly it is that liberty work with my animals stirs up in me. When I drive my flock of hundreds of sheep to new pastures with the help of my dogs, it's liberty work. I consider it "*haute école*," because I'm not just working with one other species; there are three different kinds of animals communicating with each other, a trilogy of dialogues. Even though I've done this work for thirty years, it never loses a single fraction of its magic.

Liberty work means influencing animals through direct dialogue, without force and without direct physical contact. Between the dogs and the sheep, that's liberty work with almost 50,000 pounds of live animals—without a whip, without ropes, and without any fencing. Call it magical, mysterious, or simply successful spatial communication. When I'm standing next to my gelding Berti and the flow of our liberty work stalls and sputters, I wonder how I'll find a way to redirect 1,200 pounds of horse. Luckily, I always manage to find the mistake, and knowing I'll be able to root out the problem using this step-by-step geometric language is so motivating for me.

It's important to remember that animals in work at liberty are not completely free. They need to be obedient, which means we need to be clear in providing them with boundaries and guidelines. Keeping this in mind should encourage us to communicate with care and consistently follow through with correct training.

It's a wonderful journey, obtaining a horse's consent...

...and building a partnership on that foundation.

We can easily learn the laws of their natural language from our animals, if we just listen.

Working at liberty isn't actually mysterious; there's a system you can learn and use. Despite this, I'm convinced it has a special magic and belongs in every horse's training. During liberty work, we humans learn to read space, distance, and expressive behavior. We learn to build a real dialogue without coercion, without physicality, characterized by mindfulness and empathy. And when I take these values with me into the saddle, it's a win for both of us. In my program, although the value of liberty work is immeasurable, it's also a common, everyday occurrence. Liberty work makes life so much easier, and so meaningful at the same time.

It's not about showmanship, but rather about improving the quality of life for us and our horses. For example, I can call a horse trained in liberty work out of his stall, leave him standing in the aisle, clean him, tack him up, and take him into the riding arena with very little handling. I can load him, lead him, turn him around in the pasture and scratch him, turn him out, or call him from the pasture and bring him back to the stable—all without ropes, all completely free.

This training liberates both the horse and the human being by creating a new kind of relationship, one that's entirely distinct from the traditional model of trainer and trainee. Working at liberty refines my space management and my spatial thinking, and reveals the horse's point of view to me. Liberty work is a breeding ground for comprehension, understanding, and trust. Not only does my horse trust me, but I have complete faith in him as well.

COMING TOGETHER: A FAMILY

In the kitchen, I cut some apples into slices. Then I head out to my dogs and my Berti. It's been a hard day, and I'm tired. My head is buzzing. Berti was neglected today. This happens to all of us at one time or another. I really don't have the energy to ride, but I know I can't just ignore my animals. Some running, cycling, or playing are still possible. We put our heads together, and then we set off—eight hearts, one path. We warm up: to my left, my six dogs, and on my right, my gelding Berti. If you were to ask me who my favorite animal is, I wouldn't be able to tell you, but it doesn't matter; all that matters is that I am their favorite person.

What I'm doing here is creating a family. We walk together, stop to cuddle a bit, enjoy an apple snack, play, and just walk again, casual and joyful. Such a small, effortless workout grounds me, refuels me, and balances me at the same time. A bonding game, and a meeting with friends. Sometimes it's only fifteen or twenty minutes, but when I go home, I feel refreshed and rejuvenated.

Making a horse happy with playful consistency is the foundation for a real relationship.

HABITS OF HAPPINESS

Develop a habit of making these little "escapes" with your horse. Leave your ambition at home; don't think about the next competition, lesson, obstacle, or test. Think exclusively about yourself and your horse, and stay in the moment. Dive into cultivating this habit, take time for bonding, and be fully present in moments of shared happiness. This doesn't have to be elegant or perfectly executed—the main thing is that you and your horse share positive, confident energy. Consciously create comfort zones for your horse.

Consider this quality time just as important as your other training, and make time for it. Allow your horse to ground you, read and reflect on you, and have a say in the goals you reach together. Let yourself enjoy your horse as an independent creature, as an individual with his own skills, his own visions, and his own way of communicating.

Art starts with simplicity.

Train your positive thoughts, sort out what brings you joy, and set aside time for it. Believe in your horse, and in what lies ahead for both of you.

It's never too late to start. All these family-building measures are like making deposits into a savings bank of happiness, where the time you invest comes back with interest and compound interest. Learn to take care of yourself, listen to yourself, and be patient with yourself. You're allowed to make mistakes, just as your horse is allowed to make mistakes. Learn from them, just as your horse can learn from his. Monitor your own learning curve and your own energy. And never forget: your horse will reflect your positive energy back at you.

READING, RUNNING, LISTENING

Many horse and trainer teams that came to us for help had significant problems and misunderstandings. A person's training takes time. They don't often enroll in my program simply for the sake of learning—usually something has already gone very wrong. And then, not only do they have these mistakes to fix, they're also learning an entirely new method simultaneously: no small task. Imagine wearing earbuds, and while you're listening to music, you're also trying to read a book and cross a busy road. Not only would this be difficult, but you'd probably miss some words in the book and some notes in the song—and maybe you'd walk into traffic. Simply put, it would be overwhelming. It can be a bit like this when you're working with animals. You have to be able to read your animal's expressive behavior, keep an eye on the space, and maintain a clear and correct use of language, while also following your coach's instructions. This is the ultimate form of multitasking.

Unconditional trust is based on reciprocity.

Trust is the greatest proof of love.

It takes time, not speed; it requires calm, and a willingness to address more than the "tip of the iceberg" to set our training on the right path. To reach our goals, we must be able to have a true dialogue with the horse.

IN LOVE WITH DETAILS

We have helped many human-horse teams learn to take small steps, pay attention to details, and sometimes take a step back. The moment we start to foist our human perspective on the horse, we begin to miss what is actually there. We overlook the fact that we are then arguing against ourselves, and the moment we stop using a correct means of communication, we have stopped providing the horse with correct information.

Instead, fall in love with the details; be thorough. Pay attention to the little things that a good dialogue needs in order to convey information clearly. Be your horse's comfortable and secure inside, make sure you have a safe outside, and become your horse's safe place.

DIRECTION, SPACE, AND REGULATION

During your apprenticeship in my workshop, you've come across certain terms. One of these terms is "regulation." This is a crucial ingredient for anyone who wants to be able to work with horses. Regulation is necessary to manage the functional pattern of pushing, or lack of respect for boundaries. It's the engine of life. For growing creatures to have enough stamina to withstand all the dangers, threats, and difficulties they will face, the functional pattern of pushing is crucial. You could also call it the will to survive. However, if this driving force isn't regulated, it can get out of hand, and the result will be uninhibited behavior and a lack of respect for boundaries.

On the other hand, the vitally important attachment system that allows animals to bond arises from this same pattern of pushing and seeking boundaries. This is why we can establish relationships and comfort zones, and create inner peace and relaxation. You must take care to strike the correct balance between boundaries and bonding: respect without fear, affection without dominance.

CONGRATULATIONS!

You now have a better way to understand the horse you'll be working with, some new tools to use, and some inspiration for the kind of bond you can create. You can build or repair an emotional bond and can ask uncomfortable questions in a kind way. You have learned to listen without preconceptions or emotion, and to be open to your horse's answers. You can now read your horse's expressive behavior, be it spatial, physical, or acoustic, and tell which functional pattern it belongs to. You can praise until the praise works, and you can be a safe place for your horse. You have learned to go where you want to go, stay on your line of travel, and maintain your space. You now have spatial awareness and can create your own path.

Training animals is and remains a philosophy for life, because it brings us into an inner balance, shows us how connections are forged, and equips us with a comprehensive knowledge of different means of communication. This system, my means for building happiness, won't provide you with a manual for riding a flying change or training a horse to bow. Instead, it will prepare you and your horse to establish a successful dialogue with each other, which in turn can lead to being able to ride flying changes or teaching movements like bowing. In this book, you have seen how this system has worked to resolve different kinds of problems for very different horse and human partners. We have always listened to both sides and trained both participants, as commitment isn't a one-way street. As you apply my system, you'll start to see how deep a real relationship with your horse can be, and how valuable real understanding is for this relationship. You're about to embark on an exciting, fulfilling, and creative journey with your equine partners.

You now understand how important it is to practice positive thinking: your glass is half-full. You've seen that it's never too late for a fresh start.

*"Pursue what you love,
and happiness will follow."*

—Unknown

Take your training diary and keep track of your observations, your training, your questions, and your successes. Record your progress, and your horse's progress as well. Revisit your goals, take stock of how things stand, and celebrate your small steps forward. Keep track of your horse's performance curve, have the training scale in mind, and remember you can always start over if you need to. And when you see that you've done well, give yourself a pat on the back, and gratefully accept your horse's willingness to join you on your journey. Congratulations! You're now ready to build a true bond, to create real trust and understanding, and to have a happy, harmonious relationship with your horses.

A horse doesn't trust you because of your strength, but because of your patience.

THE END

ABOUT THE AUTHOR

Communication has been the main focus of my professional life. I have had the good fortune to work with a wide variety of species: horses, sheep, dogs, and goats. As I have studied how these creatures communicate, I have learned that the basic features of communication—the laws of natural language—are based on the same principles regardless of species. My system clarifies this universal language: I've distilled what seems complex into an easy-to-use methodology, and I'm passionate about sharing this system with my students and now also with you, dear readers.

Communication is always at the core of my work, whether as a farmer, dressage rider, coach, trainer, or author. My actions are always based in language, made clear and easy. Using my system as the bedrock of training, I have created an artistic performance, and have been touring with my family and animals for the past two years. This can only work when we have the consent of our animals, when we work as a team, and when we communicate with each other in a kind and clear way. On a beautiful farm in Lower Saxony in Melle, we run HarmoniLogie Academy—a place where we teach people how to employ my system of harmonious training for both horses and dogs. This charming 150-year-old farm is also home to a flock of sheep and goats, about a dozen horses, and our hard-working dogs. We train competitive dressage and liberty work, and enjoy extensive rides through our forests.

Both by taking responsibility for the well-being of our animals, and through eavesdropping on their interactions, I've learned how important their bonds with us and each other are. Their natural laws of language create happy coexistence between them, as they work to create and maintain peace and harmony. Now you can also use their language to create this same happiness, for you and your animals!

Gratitude is the gift that makes happiness complete.

THANK YOU

Each book is a work of art, created with so many people's support. Without these people, far fewer books would ever come to fruition. This book that you hold in your hands would not have existed if not for the help of so many people. I'm honored to have this book begin with the kind words of Jessica von Bredow-Werndl, a woman who has brought her passion for, and success in, the considerate training of horses to a new level.

As a double Olympic champion in dressage, a trainer, and a mother, she understands the connections between playful consistency, team spirit, and shared goals. Thank you, Jessica. Your support is wind in my sails!

I would like to thank Birgit Bohnet, my German editor, and her team. Their sensitivity toward both the text and its author helped me to create a wonderful, artistic work. It has been a great honor for me to be able to collaborate with this professional, empathic, and talented team from Kosmos Verlag. Thank you, Birgit, it has been such a pleasure to work with you!

Photographer Anna Auerbach is a true artist; working with her on this book was a joy. Thank you, Anna; without your stunning images, this book would not be what it is!

Maureen, Suzanne, Charlotte, Luca, Gianna, Regina, Carla, Natalie, Sabine, Niclas, Jan: you have walked this path with me, and we have listened to each other and helped each other towards our goals. Each of you is a true "builder of happiness," and I truly enjoyed working with each and every one of you. I can't wait to see what the future holds for you. Thank you so much support—you've brought this book to life with your stories.

I would like to thank my friends, my team, and especially my family for your patience, the extra doses of courage and strength, the grammar checks, the coffee, and the wine that saw me through the hard parts. Most of all, I'd like to thank our horses. With loving patience, they explained to me again and again the laws of their language, answered my questions, and showed me the way. How lucky I am to be able to work with this team of two- and four-legged friends!

Thank you, from the bottom of my heart.

Yours, Anne

FURTHER READING

OTHER BOOKS YOU MIGHT BE INTERESTED IN

Jones, Janet: **Horse Brain, Human Brain.**
Instead of working *against* the horse's brain, expecting him to function in unnatural and counterproductive ways, this book provides the information needed to ride *with* the horse's brain. *Also available from Trafalgar Square Books.*

Masterson, Jim, with Reinhold, Stefanie: **Beyond Horse Massage.**
Enable your horse to perform and feel better, to overcome old limitations and restrictions and reach his full potential. *Also available from Trafalgar Square Books.*

Nölke, Marc: **Neuroathletics for Riders.**
Use the power of brain science to unlock the equestrian body's full potential. *Also available from Trafalgar Square Books.*

Wilsie, Sharon/Vogel, Gretchen: **Horse Speak: The Equine-Human Translation Guide.**
Horse Speak is not a training method or a technique to make you ride better. It is a practical system for "listening" and " talking" to horses in their language instead of expecting them to comprehend ours. *Also available from Trafalgar Square Books.*

INDEX

Page numbers in italics indicate illustrations.